Global Governance and Social Democracy

Global Governance and Social Democracy

Between Neoliberal and Authoritarian Capitalism

Nicos P. Mouzelis and Dimitri A. Sotiropoulos

BLOOMSBURY ACADEMIC
LONDON • NEW YORK • OXFORD • NEW DELHI • SYDNEY

BLOOMSBURY ACADEMIC
Bloomsbury Publishing Plc, 50 Bedford Square, London, WC1B 3DP, UK
Bloomsbury Publishing Inc, 1359 Broadway, New York, NY 10018, USA
Bloomsbury Publishing Ireland, 29 Earlsfort Terrace, Dublin 2, D02 AY28, Ireland

BLOOMSBURY, BLOOMSBURY ACADEMIC and the Diana logo are trademarks of
Bloomsbury Publishing Plc

First published in Great Britain 2024
Paperback edition published 2026

Copyright © Nicos P. Mouzelis and Dimitri A. Sotiropoulos, 2024

Nicos P. Mouzelis and Dimitri A. Sotiropoulos have asserted their right under the Copyright,
Designs and Patents Act, 1988, to be identified as Authors of this work.

Series design by Adriana Brioso
Cover image © Andriy Onufriyenko/Getty Images

Bloomsbury Publishing Plc does not have any control over, or responsibility for, any
third-party websites referred to or in this book. All internet addresses given in this
book were correct at the time of going to press. The author and publisher regret any
inconvenience caused if addresses have changed or sites have ceased to exist,
but can accept no responsibility for any such changes.

A catalogue record for this book is available from the British Library.

Library of Congress Cataloging-in-Publication Data

ISBN: HB: 978-1-3503-6116-4
PB: 978-1-3503-6117-1
ePDF: 978-1-3503-6119-5
eBook: 978-1-3503-6120-1

Typeset by Newgen KnowledgeWorks Pvt. Ltd., Chennai, India

For product safety related questions contact productsafety@bloomsbury.com.

To find out more about our authors and books visit www.bloomsbury.com
and sign up for our newsletters.

Contents

Introduction   1

Part 1   The General Framework

  1 The Coming Collapse of Capitalism?   5

  2 Global Capitalism and Its Three Subsystems: Convergence?   11

Part 2   China, the United States, and Global Governance

  3 The Rise of China   21

  4 The American Reaction   31

  5 Globalization and Global Governance   41

Part 3   From the National to the Post-National Level

  6 The Golden Years—Social Democracy (1945–75)   57

  7 Five Crises: Economic, Pandemic, Ukrainian, Taiwan, and Energy   63

  8 Social Democracy 2.0   75

Part 4   The Future of Democracy

  9 The Future of Democracy   89

10 Conclusion   95

References   103
Name Index   109
Subject Index   111

Introduction

The main aim of our book is to consider whether it is possible, within the globalized capitalism that we live, to handle effectively global risks—such as an irreversible ecological destruction, recurring pandemics, and the possibility of a nuclear world war.

Our main argument is that the scale and gravity of these risks call for innovative meta-national arrangements among three megaplayers in the world today: the USA, China, and the European Union (EU). Each of the three represents a subtype of today's global capitalism. The first is a neoliberal, the second an authoritarian, and the third a social democratic subtype of capitalism.

None of the three can manage the global risks on its own. Meanwhile, existing structures and processes of formal international cooperation, such as the G7, G20, or the climate crisis conferences (COP26 in 2021 in Glasgow, COP27 in 2022 in Sharm el-Sheikh), do not bring hopeful results. They are either too cumbersome or too loose structures and processes. If risks in the future acquire an accelerated pace, as it happened with the Covid-19 pandemic or is now happening with the climate change, a commensurate global response will become necessary.

The response cannot be ad hoc. It must be prearranged. It may be a less structured, not legally binding, three-corner arrangement among the USA, China, and the EU that, without substituting the international legal order (the United Nations (UN), international treaties, etc.), could manage global risks in time. The three megaplayers have a vested interest in meeting global risks, the solutions to which surpass the capabilities of each player. They have a motivation to act in a concerted fashion and convince, if not press, the rest of nation-states and international entities to act accordingly.

The text of our book consists of four parts. In Part 1 we try to answer two basic questions. First, is capitalism, as some left-wing thinkers believe, going to collapse quite soon? We do not believe so (Chapter 1). And second, if, as we argue, given that global capitalism consists of three capitalist subsystems (the neoliberal, the authoritarian, and the social democratic), will there be a convergence between them or not? We argue that the three subsystems need to jointly manage the largest global risks, such as climate change, pandemics, and the threat of nuclear war (Chapter 2). In Part 2 we examine the rise of China (Chapter 3) and the American reaction to its rapid economic growth and enhanced role in global politics (Chapter 4). We also examine the issue of hegemony in the context of rapid globalization (Chapter 5). Part 3 examines the development of social democracy from its "golden years" (Chapter 6) to subsequent crises: economic, pandemic, Ukrainian, and others (Chapter 7). We also deal with the EU's present meta-national situation and a new window of opportunity for social democracy ("Social Democracy 2.0," Chapter 8). Finally in Part 4 we discuss the future of democracy (Chapter 9) and we close with a summary of our book and general conclusions (Chapter 10).

In order to develop our basic arguments as clearly as possible, we have placed more detailed information in the footnotes, which the reader finds at the end of each chapter.

Part 1

The General Framework

1

The Coming Collapse of Capitalism?

After the economic crisis of 2007–8, particularly in left-wing circles, theories about the imminent collapse of capitalism have come back to the forefront.

Wolfgang Streeck

Among the different theories that we briefly discuss in this chapter, the most influential is that of Wolfgang Streeck.[1]

Streeck argues that previous theorists, from Marx to Polanyi and Sombart, have failed in their predictions. But today developments are quite different. Particularly after the opening of the world markets in the 1970s and the collapse of the Soviet Union, a unique situation has emerged. We observe interrelated trends that have led to a complete impasse: unprecedented inequalities, concentration of the global wealth to a very small minority, decreasing rates of growth in the developed world, and, at the same time, a huge public debt.[2] The abovementioned developments are linked in such a manner that it is not anymore possible to save the capitalist system. In contrast to the early postwar period, today there are no collective actors who are able to control the negative effects of financial capitalism. Trade unions are marginalized, social movements are not capable to resist global capital's strategies, and rapid individualization leads to widespread depoliticization.

In other words, for Streeck, if during the thirty golden years of social democracy (1945–75) the massive organizational base of the workers led to a balance of power between labor and capital, today a similar balance does not exist. The radical weakening of the nation-state's autonomy and its incapacity to control the movements of capital within national borders lead to a favorable situation for capital. Whenever trade unions or the state attempt to control capital, it simply moves elsewhere—in countries where social legislation is weak or nonexistent.

However, according to Streeck, the present triumph of neoliberal capitalism will soon lead to its demise. The concentration of wealth at the top leads to the weakening of demand and to permanent economic stagflation. It also leads to the decline of productive investments and the turn of investors to the financial sector. This is a sector where the creation of new financial "products" further increases inequalities and shrinks the global economy. Within this context, financial bubbles emerge which destroy small enterprises and create further unemployment. According to Streeck, all of those mentioned above create consecutive crises that, sooner rather than later, will lead to the collapse of the capitalist mode of production.

The basic weakness of Streeck's analysis is that he tries to explain future developments without taking seriously into account very powerful macro-actors who want to maintain and develop further the capitalist system. For instance, at present the United States and China are against any postcapitalist transformation. Given this, the author argues that *systemic, institutional contradictions*, irrespective of what actors do, will bring down the capitalist social order. In his analysis, however, contradictions become anthropomorphic entities that shape future developments. But, contra Streeck, it is obvious that actors are not passive products of systemic/institutional contradictions. Institutional contradictions and actors' strategies are interrelated. It is not possible to explain social change, without taking into account both *agency* and the *institutional* system.[3]

In order to make the abovementioned more persuasive one can look at Marx's overall work.[4] Marx avoids Streeck's one-dimensional analysis. His analysis, in order to explain the coming revolution, takes into account both *system contradictions* and *class struggles*. More specifically, as technologies (in Marxist terms, the forces of production) change rapidly, there is a growing contradiction between forces of production and the institution of private property. As the abovementioned contradiction grows, the proletariat acquires gradually class consciousness and is massively organized. It is precisely this articulation between collective actors and systemic contradictions which one does not see in Streeck's analysis. If, however, we bring back collective actors, then we think that it is surely premature to talk about an imminent capitalist collapse. Of course, one can argue that capitalism can change. Particularly during the pandemic period, global capitalism has become less neoliberal.[5] We might see the emergence of more powerful, political mechanisms that may attenuate the anarchic functioning of global markets. To repeat, capitalism will not survive forever, but its demise is not around the corner.[6]

Immanuel Wallerstein

Similar difficulties one finds in another theory, which predicts the collapse of capitalism, are that of Immanuel Wallerstein.[7]

The author considers that due to globalization, in the developed world the cost of labor increases and capital moves to the periphery where labor is cheap. Investments in the periphery, however, particularly in the developing countries, lead to conditions that are not favorable for the further development of capitalism—since wages go up and profits decrease. In such cases, the state tends not to cover anymore expenses related to the basic infrastructure of the enterprise. And when profits disappear, the entrepreneur has no more interest to invest further. In other terms, at some point the move to the periphery where labor is cheap stops. There is no more space for further capitalist exploitation. At this point, according to Wallerstein, we will witness the collapse of capitalism and the emergence of a postcapitalist mode of production.

In Wallerstein's theory, there is so much emphasis on systemic constraints that micro- and macro-agents are portrayed as puppets having no possibility of reacting to the "iron laws" of systemic contradictions. Since at present trade unions and social movements do not have anymore the capacity to overthrow the status quo, systemic antinomies will lead to the desired goal, to the collapse of capitalism. Obviously, what this type of reasoning ignores is that since the collapse of the Soviet regime, those who control the means not only of production, but also of domination and of mass persuasion, can find ways to revive profit making. More specifically, profits do not derive only from the exploitation of the periphery. Financial capitalism in the capitalist center creates a system that generates huge profits for those who own multinationals—particularly Big Tech giants like Amazon and Google often generate higher profits than medium-sized nation-states.[8] In such a situation, wages may improve without undermining further investments and profits.[9]

To conclude, Wallerstein's idea that capitalism is going to collapse because the scarcity of cheap labor will reduce the possibility for profit is wrong. As human needs are multiplying, there will be new markets, new investments, and new opportunities for profit.

Other Theories

Streeck's and Wallerstein's theories, briefly examined earlier, refer to systemic contradictions that will lead to the end of capitalism. Other theories predicting its end face similar problems. For instance, Alain Badiou's "The Communist Hypothesis"[10] defines the future communist emancipation in a negative manner. He argues that future communism will be different from the Soviet and fascist models.[11] Moreover, it will reject traditional values and institutions. But the means of achieving them are not mentioned. There is no reference to *who* will bring about communism and *how* the future communism is going to come about.

In another well-known analysis, the approach of Michael Hardt and Antonio Negri,[12] strategies are mentioned but are vague. According to their theory, globalization increases inequalities and the peripheralization of the poor.

This will lead to the emergence of a global popular force that will undermine the "empire." But there is no analysis of how this will happen. The conceptual framework is similar to that of theories on populism which are based on "the people versus the establishment" struggles.[13] These are theories that see the people as a collective macro-actor who will bring about the desired transformation. However, the mechanisms leading to this transformation are not examined. In contrast to the above, David Harvey[14] refers to collective actors: to nongovernmental organizations (NGOs), social movements, trade unions, and left-wing political parties—all of which should have one major goal, the revolutionary takeover of the state, leading to a postcapitalist situation. In this case, however, we have a list of actors but there is no mention of how they relate to each other and how they will become powerful enough to overthrow capitalism.

Finally, all theorists discussed earlier do not take into account the extraordinary rise of China. As we will argue in Chapter 3, the Chinese giant, via the Silk Road, invests massively in different regions of the world. In today's China, the combination of a dynamic capitalist economy and a developmentally oriented state allows foreign and Chinese entrepreneurs to operate in a way that does not undermine productivity—provided, of course, that they do not try to change the communist status quo.

The hope of some Western democrats that rapid development has already created a Chinese middle class that, sooner or later, will press for an opening of the political system is not realistic. It is true of course that the rapid growth of the Chinese economy has created huge inequalities, not only at the top but also in the middle of China's social structure.[15] But the Chinese middle classes, unlike what happened elsewhere, did not try to change the communist state apparatus. Since the communist political elite controls very effectively the army, the trade unions, the media, and all ethnic minorities, there is no serious challenge to its domination. The elite legitimizes its quasi-totalitarian rule by the reduction of absolute poverty, the development of a Confucian ideology focusing on family values, and a rising nationalism based on the extraordinary transformation of an erstwhile developing country into a global superpower.

To conclude, capitalism is not an ideal system that will survive forever. But given at present the dominance of global capitalism, a collapse is not going to come soon. It will be with us for a very long time.

Notes

1 See Streeck (2014) and (2016).
2 See Piketty (2014).
3 Streeck's analysis reminds one of Parsons's conceptual framework (1951). The father of modern sociological theory tries to explain social change by showing how systemic contradictions shape social developments. He does not show how actors reproduce and change institutional arrangements. The direction of change is from the institutional system to the actor rather than the other way around (Mouzelis 1997).
4 In some of his works Marx gives more emphasis on class struggles, whereas in other texts (the so-called, by Althusser, "scientific texts") the focus is on systemic

contradictions that unavoidably will lead to a capitalist collapse. However, if one looks at Marx's work as a whole, there is an *articulation* between institutional systemic contradictions and collective actors. For more recent theories on the articulation between systemic antinomies and social actors, see Mouzelis (1997).

5 In the advanced capitalist economies, the state funded basic research, enforced safety regulations, and provided vaccines. It facilitated the transformation of laboratory research outcomes into suitable products to fight Covid-19 as soon as the pandemic struck (see Irwin 2020).

6 In a more recent text, Streeck (2017) is concerned less with systemic contradictions of the present crisis and more with the impact globalization has on the nation-state. The rapid decline of its autonomy undermines the efforts to resist the storm of neoliberal capitalism. As the nation-state weakens, the economic prevails over the political. In this situation, those peripheralized turn to the populist parties that are for a de-globalization that will lead to a return of an autonomous nation-state. The author, by using Gramsci's term "interregnum" (2017: 14–18), considers it as a transitional period, probably as a step before the collapse of the capitalist order.

7 See Wallerstein (2013).

8 See Krippner (2005) on the financialization of American capitalism.

9 For more recent books criticizing and predicting the end of capitalism, see Oli Mould (2018) and Tom Jackson (2021).

10 See Badiou (2008, 2009, and 2010).

11 See Badiou and Gauchet (2016).

12 See Hardt and Negri (2000, 2004).

13 See Laclau (2005).

14 See Harvey (2010).

15 See Jain-Chandra et al. (2018).

2

Global Capitalism and Its Three Subsystems: Convergence?

The global economic system is clearly neoliberal in the sense that political control mechanisms of global market developments are weak. But after the collapse of the Soviet system, capitalism spreads everywhere. It consists of three capitalist subsystems: the authoritarian whose main representative is China, the neoliberal represented by the United States, and the EU's social democratic one.[1] The three subsystems have different logics, in terms of both their internal functioning and the way they relate to the global system.[2]

The Authoritarian Capitalist Subsystem

Once China fully entered the world markets, it privatized some of its highly inefficient public enterprises and welcomed foreign investments—provided that investors did not criticize or oppose the dominance of the Chinese communist party and its overall handling of the economy.[3] The abovementioned changes led to a spectacular economic growth that increased inequalities,[4] particularly in the urban centers. But at the same time, absolute poverty was considerably reduced. For the first time in Chinese history peasants did not die from hunger during draught periods.

Of course, rapid economic development led to the growth of the middle classes. But, unlike the Southern Korean case,[5] this did not lead to a gradual political liberalization. In South Korea rapid export-oriented growth and the development of a politically oriented middle class undermined the military government, leading thus to a liberal parliamentary system.[6] The same happened in several Latin American regimes that experienced liberalization after an alteration between military and civilian governments.[7] But the Chinese case is very different. Given that the party controls the army, trade unions, ethnic minorities, and the media, the system is extremely difficult to change. As far as ideology is concerned, the Chinese president tries to educate the youth into a system of values based on a mixture of orthodox Marxism and the Confucian tradition—a tradition that stresses the importance of family values and social order. To the above one should also mention that the legitimation of the Chinese regime has been strengthened by the extraordinary economic growth, by the millions of people who moved above the line of absolute poverty, and by the growth of patriotism that the Chinese interventions in the South China Sea and elsewhere have created.[8]

The Neoliberal Capitalist Subsystem

In the case of the neoliberal subsystem,[9] its dominant ideology stresses that fewer political market controls lead to the production of more wealth. Wealth, via a "trickle-down" process, spreads to the social base.[10] However, as many critics have pointed out, the wealth produced does not always spread to the social base. One observes instead huge inequalities that systematically undermine the welfare state.[11] Particularly during Donald Trump's presidency, neoliberal policies were strengthened: reduction of taxes on enterprises and the wealthy, weakening of governmental/bureaucratic controls, and a further shrinking of welfare services (see Chapter 4).

Of course, with President Biden we observe radical changes. There is a move to more progressive policies. Huge resources have been used not only for infrastructural projects but also for helping families, small enterprises, and the unemployed. There are as well serious attempts at reducing inequalities by raising the corporate tax and fighting tax evasion. In other terms, there is a shift from neoliberal to more interventionist policies.

However, it would be wrong to see Biden's changes as a transformation of the United States into a social democratic society. The persistent huge inequalities, the power of American multinationals, the possibility of Trump's return to power in the presidential election of 2024, the widespread culture that emphasizes the urge to reach economic success, the legitimation of quasi-universal gun ownership, the weakness of the welfare state, and Trump's massive appeal to the voters blur the image of post-Trump United States. All the above, despite Biden's generosity and his decisive state interventionism, do not make the United States a social democratic capitalist subsystem.[12]

The Social Democratic Capitalist Subsystem

During social democracy's thirty "golden years" (1945–75), social democratic parties, mainly in North-West Europe, managed to govern and spread civic, political, economic, and social rights to the societal base.[13] They combined balanced economic growth with a developed welfare system and a stable regime of representative democracy.[14] In other terms, during its early postwar period, social democracy achieved, for the first time in the long history of capitalism, a socioeconomic system with a human face (see Chapter 6). A system without China's authoritarian features or the United States' persistent lack of social rights in the health, welfare, and educational sphere.

Social democracy went through a severe crisis in the late 1970s. As we will argue more extensively in later chapters, there were several factors that led to an impasse. But we think that the most important was the opening of the world markets that enabled capital to transcend national boundaries moving to countries where taxation was low and labor protection laws were weak or nonexistent. To put it in other terms, globalization undermined the autonomy of the nation-state. European social democratic parties, in order to survive, had to some extent to adopt neoliberal values and practices. For some social democrats, that was treason. For others it was the only way to survive in a new context within which Keynesian policies were leading to stagflation.

Finally, it was realized that the only way to achieve again social democratic goals was in a broader post-national space—that of the eurozone, provided the latter moved rapidly to become a more integrated entity. The process of integration was difficult. For a variety of reasons, several EU member states were reluctant to lose part of their autonomy. The tension between centrifugal and centripetal tendencies was so strong that in the early 2010s many observers were predicting the union's collapse.[15] This did not happen. Gradually integration increased to the extent that Europhobes or anti-European leaders, like Le Pen and Salvini, stopped threatening an exit.

The main steps toward more unity were the creation of the euro and the realization that a precondition for its success was the strengthening of democratic institutions. A second step was Draghi's statement that the European Central Bank (ECB) will do "whatever it takes" to save the euro.[16]

The next breakthrough was that during the pandemic crisis, we see the creation of the Resilience and Recovery Facility (RRF), which will help mainly, but not only, the less developed EU member states. That move aimed to reduce the North-South divide. Finally, there was an arrangement that enabled the union to borrow money with favorable terms helping thus member states accordingly, which was another decisive step at integration.

As a result of the abovementioned successive breakthroughs, the EU ceased to be only a huge market. The EU was not just a free market permeated by neoliberal economic principles, but retained and even strengthened social democratic features. It was transformed gradually into a powerful political and social configuration, a key player in the global arena. Of course, in comparison with other key players, the armed forces of EU member states are less important. But the union has the capacity to be the major mediator between China and the United States. And this because of EU's goal of "strategic autonomy." Merkel, Macron, and other leaders have pointed out that American interests do not always coincide with European ones. Taking into account the above, the EU, after its crisis, emerges as a power that is in the process of realizing its past achievements, but this time on a meta-national level (see Chapter 8).

The Issue of Convergence

For some observers, the three capitalist subsystems will gradually converge. For instance, some believe that the Chinese one will gradually open up—as its rapid growth has created an important middle class that will press for democratization. But China's ruling communist party has stronger roots than any other authoritarian regime. The idea of a gradual democratization is not persuasive. Neither is the argument that at some point excessive state regulation and ideological regimentation will undermine China's present rise.

Both the abovementioned theories, as well as the theories of Streeck and Wallerstein that we examined in the previous chapter, do not take seriously into account that the rise of China has brought about a tectonic change of relations between "the West and the rest." There is a new balance of power, which is irreversible. This does not mean the "sinicization" of the world. The tripolar system of the authoritarian, neoliberal, and social democratic capitalist subsystems will not converge. Of course, the importance of each can vary. For the moment the Chinese subsystem is rapidly rising, but the American is still dominant. The interdependence of the three subsystems means that they will continue having different trajectories—each one needing the other two for its reproduction.

The real issue, however, is whether China and the United States will cooperate or will follow, as they do now, a confrontation policy. This means that global risks, like pandemics and ecological destruction, cannot be handled by contemporary states, each operating on a self-isolation mode. We will try to show this by looking at the vaccination problem. During the pandemic crisis in 2020–22 the vaccination problem has been dealt in such a way that a definite global solution was not possible. In the developed world, vaccines were available almost to all, whereas in the so-called third world they were not. In poor countries the number of deaths was growing rapidly. It was impossible to deal with the problem effectively if one followed such a fragmented, uncoordinated strategy. The contributions of the G7, G20, and other international organizations were not enough. The chasm between the developed countries and those of the global periphery grew. The World Health Organization (WHO) had hoped to fully vaccinate 70 percent of the global population by June 2022. But by August 2022 very few of the world's 82 poorest countries had achieved the 70 percent target. In many of the latter countries only a third of the population was vaccinated.

If the pandemic resurges, as the problem is global, the only way to deal with it is by mobilizing global actors. Actors who have the economic, political, and geopolitical power to bridge the divide between the rich and the poor. There are two such actors: the United States and China. They produce nuclear weapons in an endless race for dominance. If, however, they decide to agree *simultaneously* to reduce their military budget by a small fraction, there would be enough resources for providing vaccines to everybody, in case new pandemics emerge.

One may think that this is utopian. Is the abovementioned proposal impossible to implement? We think it is possible if one considers that it can be a *win-win* game. For two reasons: first, the balance of power between China and the United States will not change since none of the two will become poorer. Second, both will increase what Bourdieu calls their "cultural capital." They may perhaps become model leaders who will have saved the planet from an invisible enemy.

Needless to say, the same argument applies to other global problems, such as the project of decarbonization that requires huge resources. A project that at present moves so slowly that an overall irreversible ecological catastrophe is a reasonable possibility. It is time to realize that as globalization advances rapidly, it is impossible to cope with global risks without the cooperation between the superpowers that use vast resources for the creation of more and more sophisticated weapons of global destruction.

Finally, as we will explain in greater detail later, the EU, which obviously is not a superpower in geopolitical terms, can contribute to a project like the one proposed earlier since the union has decided to follow a "strategy of autonomy" on various issues vis-à-vis the American and the Chinese superpowers.

Both Merkel and Macron pointed out that the interests of the United States do not always coincide with those of the EU. They clearly did not agree with Biden's ideological crusade against China. Merkel claimed that Germany wanted to have good relations with both China and Russia (of course before Putin's invasion in Ukraine). The EU chooses cooperation rather than frontal confrontation. For those who want to cope with global risks, there is no doubt that aggression not only by Trump but also by Biden (see Chapter 4) will be met by China's reaction. This is a formula leading to another cold war and perhaps even to a third world war.

In conclusion, it is deduced that the three capitalist subsystems will persist in the years to come. The hegemony problems, as we will argue in Chapter 5, will not of course disappear. But given the change in the power balance that globalization has led to, not in the short but in the medium term, China may become the next hegemon. Whatever happens, the gradual social democratization of the EU can render it an arbitrator between the two superpowers. It will exercise global influence based less on its geopolitical power and more on its civilizational and humanistic traditions.

Notes

1 Our typology of three capitalist subsystems is not based on the complementarity of different subsystems found within each capitalist economy and the coordination among them (or lack thereof). That, as is well known, is the typology of varieties of capitalism by Hall and Soskice (2001). Rather, our typology recognizes that today capitalism is a global system, within which three subsystems may be discerned, on the basis of variable relations between state and capitalist economy.

2 The typology of the three capitalist subsystems is an ideal typical construction. In the sense that, following M. Weber (see Albrow 1990) it is a conceptual tool with the help of which one can explore empirically different variations of each type.

3 See Pierson, Rithmire, and Tsai (2021).

4 China is rapidly approaching the huge US inequalities (see Therborn 2001). But inequalities are not as bad as ten years ago (see *Economist*, October 2, 2021).

5 In South Korea a dictatorial regime followed successfully an export-oriented policy. Economic growth created a middle class that at some point overthrew the military regime.

6 See Pirie (2008).

7 See Mouzelis (1986).

8 Putting the Chinese authoritarian regime in broader macrohistorical framework, in other parts of the word, state elites pursued administrative modernization along with economic liberalization in what turned out to be "revolution from above" (Trimberger 1978). In the late nineteenth century, Japanese, Russian, and Turkish autocrats, in varying degrees and forms, promoted capitalism. That, however, was a type of "autocratic capitalism" (Frieden and Rogowski 2014), a model perhaps revisited, under very different circumstances and with different aims, in China at the turn of the twentieth into the twenty-first century (*China's authoritarian capitalism*, being the first of the three subsystems in our analysis of current global capitalism).

9 Liberalism, as developed by thinkers in the nineteenth century, was a theory against authoritarian regimes and political oppression more generally. For instance, John Stuart Mill, a major theorist of classical liberalism, argued that a precondition for the development of individual rights is the freedom of markets. However, later he realized that unregulated markets lead to growing inequalities. Therefore, he changed his mind. He stressed that state intervention is necessary for avoiding the injustice that economic liberalism generates.

10 See Friedman (1962).

11 See Milanovic (2016).

12 As the nineteenth century turned into the twentieth century, the British model of capitalism prevailed in the sense that European states imitated the British strategy of pursuing free trade and setting a predetermined exchange rate against gold for exchanging national currencies (the gold standard), as well as colonial expansion into new lands (e.g., the scramble for Africa). New imperialism coupled with economic globalization marked the peak of this laissez-faire period before the First World War. It was a period in which economies from all over the world, including countries as different as Australia, Canada, and the southern cone countries of Latin America, participated in the international economic order through exporting primary products and obtaining loans from European banks (Frieden and Rogowski 2014). The kind of economic integration on a world scale did not last long after the First World War. The play of largely unbound capitalism would acquire center stage, once more, in the very different post–Cold War context at the end of the twentieth century, the heyday of *neoliberal capitalism* (the second of the three subsystems, in our analysis of current global capitalism).

13 See, among others, Korpi (1983), Rueda (2007), and Bailey (2009).

14 See Esping-Andersen (1990).

15 See, for instance, Krastev (2020). See also Gillingham (2016).

16 European Central Bank's president Mario Draghi, in a speech delivered on July 26, 2012, promised that the bank would do "whatever it takes" to overcome the European sovereign debt crisis of the time.

Part 2

China, the United States, and Global Governance

3

The Rise of China

After Mao's death, Deng Xiaoping succeeded to move away from the previous Soviet-like type development.[1] A development that, despite some achievements,[2] led to chaos and extreme poverty. Deng managed to create a system that combined a capitalist base with a developmentally oriented state. The communist state allowed a relative autonomy of foreign and indigenous corporations, provided that they did not oppose the state and its regulatory role. Despite such limitations, China achieved a remarkable growth.[3] Its entrepreneurs have enough autonomy to operate effectively, increasing productivity and profits. It is for this reason that most foreign companies do not accept President Biden's recommendations that American companies should not invest in China and that those that are already investing should return home. Obviously, despite Western efforts China has become a superpower that threatens America's hegemony.

These do not mean that the Chinese giant is soon to play the hegemonic role. Technologically America is still ahead. For instance, many exports such as high technology machines are produced by American corporations having branches in China. Most probably, despite China's attempts to "steal"[4] American innovations, the US advantage in scientific research and innovation, theoretical and applied, will continue. Moreover, in the geopolitical sphere, according to Johnson,[5] the United States will keep their hegemony because of the network of American military bases all over the globe. Gindin and Panitch argue that the American hegemony will continue because in the postwar period the basic rules of the capitalist economy were imposed by the Americans.[6] Mitter claims that China has adapted to the globalized world economy, but it has also obliged the rest of the world to partially adapt to its own economic needs and will probably continue to do so.[7] Clifford believes that in the context of rapidly evolving technological innovation, China would prefer to sustain its cardinal role in the supply chains of the world and participate in global scientific endeavors.[8]

Of course, China cannot keep its very high growth rates, even though the Chinese economy expanded by 6.3 percent year-on-year in the second quarter of 2023.[9] Neither has China avoided steps backward.[10] But, overall, it adopts systematically developmental reforms such as the reduction of the number of inefficient state enterprises,[11] the decentralization of state controls in agriculture, the president's fight against kleptocracy, the regulation of Big Techs, and so on. In other terms, the communist elites know that, in order for their country to continue its economic dynamism, they will have to develop new strategies.

For instance, China is creating megacities that are connected by superfast trains. This is supposed to increase productivity and, therefore, further development. Moreover, one observes the rapid rise of tech companies focusing on innovation in the areas of artificial intelligence (AI),[12] semiconductors, and big data processing. Another fundamental change is the shift of focus of the Chinese government to areas away from China's coasts. Previously reforms focused only on coastal cities where goods could easily reach ports. Meanwhile, other areas in the mainland became also important, a trend reinforced during the Ukrainian crisis. The Western sanctions against Russia affected China as well. As a response the latter tried systematically to create more techs at home.[13]

Finally, another important dimension of China's development is that its huge global investments via the Silk Road were also oriented to poor countries.[14] Particularly in Africa its economic role is dominant. In many cases China's loans are "strategic." For instance, the Chinese already have a military base in Djibouti at the Horn of Africa. They also want to establish a naval presence in Equatorial Guinea. If this is realized, it will give China a foothold in the Atlantic side of Africa. China's spread of its model has led to a new situation. The continuing of American hegemony will coexist with a global change consisting of a shrinking of the Western political influence and the expanding of the non-Western one. We think that this fundamental division is irreversible.

In the social sphere, given China's rapidly expanding economy, inequalities are growing fast, particularly at the top.[15] As far as the base of the social pyramid is concerned, during the last decade the prosperity gap between the rural and urban population became narrower. At the same time absolute poverty has almost disappeared. As to the middle classes they have also improved their position. When the World Bank updates its classification, China will be in the "high-income" group countries.[16] This is not surprising since China's global investments continue, while digitalization advances fast. Before the Ukrainian crisis, supply chains worked reasonably well and new technologies boosted productivity.

Looking at the regime as a whole, the Chinese Communist Party (CCP) controls the army, the police,[17] the judiciary, and the press. Concerning civil society, after the Tiananmen square violent repression, social movements are weak, recalcitrant minorities are forcefully "reeducated," and dissidents are imprisoned.

In the past, political regimes of China collapsed in periods of large-scale social and economic transformation, as it happened with the Manchu-led Qing dynasty in 1911 and the regimes that succeeded it until 1949. Preventing regime collapse and personal fall from power has since been the prime concern of the Chinese communist leadership.[18]

Moreover, intraorganizational factionalism and the traditional opaqueness of decision-making within the ruling party have made China's leadership sensitive to unpredictable challenges to its power. "The fundamental goal of the CCP is to stay in power. People ask why a ruling autocratic communist party would provide the business class room to grow. The answer is that wealth creation underpins the longevity of CCP rule."[19] In brief, control of the country is the top priority of contemporary Chinese leadership.

The leadership of China would want to join any new international arrangement, as long as the arrangement would contribute to the regime's stability and to its own hold on power. In the long run, managing frictions with the United States and Europe would allow China to grow further and prosper, thus consolidating its domestic political legitimacy. It would also create a more predictable environment for China's investment projects in the economically developed and developing worlds. All the same it would help construct a public image of China as a rising world hegemon that would be less tarnished by alarming moves, such as throwing around its weight in Southeast Asia and the Pacific, or compromising the security of world telecommunications (through TikTok), or infringing on intellectual property rights of Western companies. Thus, for the Chinese leadership, joining and adhering to international arrangements among the mega-powers would be useful to serve its own political interests (see Chapter 5).

As far as President Xi's future is concerned, he tries to become the for-life leader of China. Given his growing power, he will probably succeed. It is not therefore surprising that in the Sixth Plenum of the 19th Central Committee of the CCP (November 2021), Xi Jinping was declared as the successor of Mao Zedong and Deng Xiaoping. Moreover, particularly after the 20th National Congress of the CCP in October 2022, Xi managed to place in high posts his friends.[20] And his aggressive policy in the South China Sea[21] leads to the strengthening of patriotism and the further legitimation of his rule.

Still, as Cai Xia has argued,[22] Xi may have some weaknesses. While Xi projects internationally an image of a competent leader, his record has been very mixed. He has steered China toward higher economic growth and economic expansion in the world (investments in Africa, "Belt and Road Initiative" in Asia and Europe). However, his strongman tactics at home is an underlying, potential threat to China's economic success and the legitimacy of the CCP's regime. Xi has alienated political allies in the party leadership, has suppressed critical voices in Chinese society, and has clumped down on selected Chinese businessmen.

Instead of further liberalizing the Chinese economy, Xi has reintroduced heavy state interference in private businesses. Such a policy choice was only partly derived from Xi's drive to contain corruption. It was also part of his larger strategy to control the private business sector of China, which, under previous economic reforms, had acquired a relative autonomy from the CCP.

On foreign policy issues, China has found itself under frequent diplomatic and economic attacks by President Biden, on the grounds of violation of human rights, wrongful business practices, and corruption. China has responded with attacks against the United States. Above all it has also intensified its military presence in the waters of South China Sea and has not ruled out a military attack to put Taiwan under Chinese rule. If Xi faces political threats at home or economic challenges abroad, he may attack Taiwan.

Having restricted pluralism in his immediate decision-making circle, Xi may not have full and reliable information on his available policy options in both the domestic and foreign affairs fronts. He himself rose to power primarily through family reputation and political party connections rather than through exhibiting competence or expertise. This is reflected, for instance, in the inefficient manner in which the Chinese leadership handled the outbreak of the Covid-19 crisis in 2020 in Wuhan and again in 2022 in selected cities (e.g. the lockdown of Shanghai and other cities).

In the past, China was able to overcome various hurdles, owing to the merits of collective leadership and decision-making. Under Xi, the concentration of power in the hands of one man has been immense. Such concentration means that inefficiencies, delays, and inactivity associated with the functioning of leadership are not always overcome. It may also mean that deficiencies of leadership are traced back to the deficiencies of a single person, the leader. This tendency is particularly consequential, if the leader also engages in micromanagement, as Xi does, leaving little room to others to implement policy decisions as they see fit. Indeed, Xi demands a very high degree of loyalty from others on large and small issues the management of which he personally oversees. He has also reversed earlier trends toward separating the Chinese state administration from the CCP. And—in contrast to his predecessors in power—he has arranged to serve a third term as president.

Despite all the above, the authoritarian aspects of the Chinese regime may be weaker than those of the Soviet Union, because China's capitalist economic base, as already mentioned, gives more autonomy to both Chinese and foreign entrepreneurs, autonomy that obviously did not exist in the Soviet system. It is precisely this feature that explains China's rapid growth and, contrary to some critics, the permanence of its authoritarian structure. Of course, recently communist authorities are regulating more tightly the private sector.[23] But the Chinese president tries to strike a balance between state regulation and entrepreneurial autonomy—since the private sector leads to rapid growth.

It is worth mentioning here that one can see three stages of Xi's strategy in relation to economic development. *First*, before the 20th Congress of the CCP, the focus was on rapid growth. *Second*, after the Congress ended, the emphasis was on more strict regulation of the private sector and the spread of the produced wealth downward ("common prosperity"). The CCP also emphasized further "modernization" based on Marxism and on Chinese culture and values. This led to an exit of some foreign corporations, particularly those that did not have already large-scale investments. Most remained because of the huge Chinese market. But, overall, the rate of growth declined considerably. As to foreign policy, the focus was on the development of the armed forces and of advanced technologies. *Third*, after the abrupt end of the zero Covid-19 policy and the ensuing massive spread of the disease in a context where hospitals and doctors were unable to cope, there was a new opening.[24] Chinese authorities adopted a more friendly approach toward foreign investors and eschewed a strong confrontation policy toward the United States and its allies. Going further toward this direction the Chinese president decided to become *mediator* between Iran and South Arabia. It was a successful move.

President Xi wanted to continue by contributing to an end of the Ukrainian war. He visited Putin and, among other issues, discussed the possibility of starting negotiations aiming at finding a solution to the ongoing war. He produced a twelve-point paper on how to start negotiations. The American reaction was negative. This reaction meant that the war should continue till Ukraine, with the support of the West, defeats Putin.

Geopolitically Putin's invasion in Ukraine changed the global power system. The United States and the EU imposed serious sanctions to Russia.[25] As a result, the Russian president turned to China for aid and political support. There is no doubt that the Chinese-Russian alliance enhances China's geopolitical position. Given Russia's weak economy, the country will more or less become a satellite of the Chinese giant. The latter will support Putin but without breaking his economic relations with the EU. Moreover, although China refused to condemn the Russian invasion of Ukraine, Xi proposed negotiations leading to a Russian withdrawal. But whatever the result of the invasion, China wants to avoid the type of polarization that Putin would prefer.

Finally, in an important joint statement the two leaders stressed their opposition to NATO's expansion and their rejection of Western interference into their internal affairs. Still, in a more positive manner the statement supports global cooperation rather than confrontation.[26]

To conclude, China's extraordinary rise has changed the world order. It definitely challenges the American hegemony. But despite its alliance with Russia, the Chinese leadership tries to avoid direct confrontation with the United States. Socially, despite huge inequalities, Chinese citizens during the last decade improved their socioeconomic situation. Politically the communist party's total control of the army, the media, and civil society stabilizes the regime. Geopolitically its model spreads rapidly in Asia and elsewhere in the periphery of the capitalist system.

As far as the Ukrainian crisis is concerned, irrespective of success or failure of the negotiations, China is the only power to force Putin to forget his grandiose revisionist policies. The Chinese president above all wants stability and may decide to put an end to the phantasies of his dependent partner. He could thus contribute more to move the planet from the present destructive polarization to cooperation. As mentioned in this chapter, Xi considers himself being at the same level as Mao Zedong and Deng Xiaoping. If he achieves to tame Putin, he may move to a higher level than Mao and Deng. To put it in other words and sum up, we think that at present it is in China's interest to lead the superpowers from the present confrontation to global cooperation.

Notes

1 See Dikötter (2022), Kirshner (2012), and Hung (2009).
2 Mao's strategy was disastrous, but it contributed to some extent to the development of industry.
3 An indication of China's economic development is that China's entrance in the world markets, unlike that of Russia during the same period, led to rapid growth. Comparing the two countries during the 1990–2017 period, the Russian "shock therapy" led to rapid economic decline. During the same time, the Chinese economy grew almost sevenfold.
4 However, one must take into account that today, via digital technologies, the monopolization of scientific knowledge is very difficult (see *The Economist*, March 7, 2018). For the rapid expansion of knowledge today, see Romers (1990).
5 See Johnson (2007).
6 See Gindin and Panitch (2012).
7 See Mitter (2016).
8 See Clifford (2021).
9 See *Trading Economics*, China GDP Annual Growth Rate, https://tradingeconom ics.com/china/gdp-growth-annual.
10 For instance, Evergrande's huge debt threatened to cripple the property sector. Two other factors, which undermined rapid development, were the strict rules in order to fight Covid-19 and the attempt to reshape and control more the Chinese

private sector. But despite the above some corporations are still thriving (see *The Economist*, August 13, 2022).

11 The remaining state enterprises continue to underperform. But given their importance in key sectors (steal, coal, transport, electricity, telecommunications) they are supported by the government. It should be mentioned here that we see a type of hybrid model of state and private property organizations that are successful (Clifford 2021). Big Techs generally are helped, particularly if they operate in areas considered by the government as important.

12 China has recently tried to develop a very advanced AI sector. It moves rapidly. One third of the top AI experts are Chinese, although only one tenth work in China. In terms of AI publications the country is first, but fewer papers are peer reviewed (see *The Economist*, January 22, 2022). Concerning the huge number of Chinese students who study outside their country, most of them return home (*The Economist*, November 27, 2021).

13 See Clifford (2021).

14 Initially some of China's investments to poor countries were for geopolitical reasons. At present they are more focused on infrastructure work. This is better for both lenders and borrowers (see *The Economist*, February 25, 2023).

15 On the huge inequalities at the top of the social pyramid, see Therborn (2021).

16 See *The Economist*, February 5, 2022.

17 The police control is reinforced by "the neighborhood country," people are mobilized to police each other! (see *The Economist*, November 12, 2022). Moreover the police controls Chinese refugees abroad by punishing their families living in China, among other methods (see *The Economist*, February 18, 2023).

18 See Mitter (2016).

19 See Clifford (2021).

20 A recent adviser that the Chinese president admires is Wang Huning. A Chinese academic who lived in the United States and sees weak points not only in America but also in China. Although he thought that authoritarianism was necessary earlier, he thinks that today the country should move to a more liberal system. By "liberal" he does not mean the end of the one-party system, but a more flexible one. At present he is one of the seven members of the Politburo Standing Committee, a very powerful ruling body.

21 In the South China Sea, countries like the Philippines reacted to China's attempt to dominate the area by, among other policies, turning rocks into artificial islands on which military bases are built. Moreover, China is demanding the right to veto the Association of Southeast Asian Nations (ASEAN) members' naval exercisers with foreign powers. It wants to keep foreigners out from joint oil and gas exploitations. This type of bullying enhances Chinese patriotism.

22 See Xia (2022).

23 See *The Economist*, November 20, 2021.

24 Concerning China's health system, in 2009 government unveiled a plan that was supposed to provide universal health care. By 2021 more than 95 percent of the population had some form of government-financed health insurance. Despite the above, after the end of the zero Covid-19 policy, the extraordinary spread of the disease showed that the health system was very inadequate (see *The Economist*, December 24, 2022).

25 As far as exports were concerned the problem was not serious. Russia's exports to China and India solved the problem. As far as China's recovery is concerned, it came earlier than expected. Growth has moved from 3 percent to 5–6 percent. But given that today's growth is based on consumption, this could lead to inflation (see *The Economist*, February 11, 2023).

26 Despite recent reforms, migrants moving to the towns remain second-class citizens (see *The Economist*, September 24, 2022).

4

The American Reaction

Donald Trump's Strategy

Considering the US-China relations, it is important first to examine Trump's strategy not only against China but also more generally. Inside the United States, while he was president, Trump followed a neoliberal policy: reduction of taxation for corporations and the rich and decreasing state regulation.[1] Under his presidency, economic inequality worsened in the United States.[2] Trump's policies also increased social inequalities affecting women, migrants, and ethnic minorities.[3] Externally he adopted a protectionist policy that not only reduced the global production of resources, but also slowed the growth of the American economy. Protectionism hurt world trade without giving the United States a significant lasting advantage over its global economic competitors, such as China and the EU. The unavoidable reaction of the countries that were hurt by the imposition of American custom duties made the products imported in the United States more expensive.

Another policy that weakened American hegemony was Trump's partial distance from the EU and NATO. Trump particularly detested commitments of the United States to its allies in Europe. Concerning the defense of Europe, he thought that American responsibilities, in the context of NATO, should be off-loaded to European member states of the alliance. Trump's concerns were primarily economic. He wanted to cut costs, brushing aside any negative effects of such a shift would have on the status of the United States as a global power and on relations of trust among NATO member states.

The prospect of weakening US-Europe ties in the field of joint defense commitments, which eventually did not materialize, led EU authorities to realize that they cannot trust Trump in matters concerning defense. Thus,

Trump's policy strengthened the resolution of Macron to accelerate Europe's autonomy policy, since European interests are not always similar with those of the United States.

More generally, Trump started deconstructing the edifice that the United States had created after the end of the Second World War. An edifice partly based on the creation of a network of alliances supported by American economic and military aid. According to Trump, the resources used for the creation of the abovementioned network were a waste of money. Trump wanted to use resources dedicated to the NATO alliance to the benefit of US business enterprises. In his view, these resources should have been used for the further development of solely the American economy and the military forces, since it is mainly the advance of military technologies which can safeguard the US global dominance.

What the ex-president did not realize was that taking distances from the US allies did not render America "first" but the opposite. Trump's isolationist policies undermined his country's global power, whereas China's initial non-isolationist, expansive strategy rendered the country more powerful. For instance, during the Trump presidency, China expanded its military presence in the South China Sea and the Pacific Ocean.

Concerning the climate issue, Trump followed an ethnocentric policy by withdrawing from the Paris climate agreement. The Paris Agreement was signed in December 2015 by 196 states, including the United States. It aimed to limit global temperature rise to well below 2°C above preindustrial levels. To achieve this aim, specific national targets were set, but they were nonbinding. And yet the Trump administration decided in November 2020 to make the United States the first and only state to withdraw from the agreement, effecting a blow to the international accord to manage climate change. (The United States rejoined the agreement in 2021 under the Biden administration.)

Trump ignored the obvious fact that in a globalized world there are common problems and common interests. As is well known, both China and the United States are contributing enormously to the rapid carbonization process. China and the United States are the world's leaders in global carbon emissions (followed by India, Russia, and Japan). Together, China and the United States, in 2019 produced over 15 billion tons of carbon dioxide.[4] However, unlike the USA under Trump, China, which follows a policy to reduce such emissions, accepted the Paris Agreement.

One can view Trump's overall strategy as an attempt to cope with a fundamental change that globalization has created. Western economic and political power prevailed during the colonial period and later, by the rise of the United States. Even after decolonization, European powers exercised economic and diplomatic influence over many of their former colonies in Africa, South Asia, the Pacific, and elsewhere. Meanwhile, after the Second World War, the United States expanded economically around the world and also made its military presence felt on a global scale. In 2023 the United States had approximately 750 military bases outside its national borders. They were spread in eighty countries.[5] Today, however, the US economic and military global presence is under challenge. China's extraordinary growth and expansion of its model in several countries in the periphery and semi-periphery of the capitalist world is gradually undermining Western dominance.

Despite Trump's goal to "Make America Great Again" (MAGA) and render the United States "first," his policies have weakened his country's hegemonic role. His partial disconnection from previous allies (particularly the EU), his authoritarian and hectic style of governing, and his protectionist policies cast doubts about the willingness and capability of the United States to retain the driver's seat in the Western world. Longtime friends of the United States felt alienated, while foes smelled weakness. Of course, for the time being, the United States controls the global financial system. The dollar remains the main means of international transactions. But this may not last for very long. The Chinese extraordinary economic growth, the country's technological advances, and its massive infrastructural investments all over the globe may sooner or later challenge America's primacy.

Biden against China

After his assuming power in January 2021, President Biden declared that commercial relations between the United States and China will not be based anymore on "war" as during the Trump period. But on the other hand, he started an ideological crusade against the Chinese superpower. He continually stressed China's lack of democratic values and practices like the confinement of minorities in camps of "reeducation," the abolition of trade union autonomy, and the intolerance to any serious critique of the government.

In addition to those mentioned earlier, the American president supports movements and alliances that criticize the authoritarian character of the Chinese regime. There is no doubt that Biden's critique of the absence of democratic values and practices in China is correct. But it is quite obvious that the US president's ideological war is not effective in gradually democratizing the Chinese political and social order or in stopping China's further growth. It will most probably lead to an intensified confrontation that will reduce the possibilities of cooperation between the two countries. Cooperation that is necessary for dealing with global problems such as the growing ecological deterioration, the breakout of any new pandemics, and the risk of a third world war.

More generally, in a different manner than Trump, Biden is trying to cope with a profound change in the relations and the balance between the West and the rest of the world, a change that globalization has brought about. As we have already pointed out, there is a large-scale shift that has led to the weakening of the global Western dominance. A dominance that was mainly consolidated by the postwar rise of the United States. Biden may have realized but has not yet provided a stable response to the following trend: the rise of China and the willingness of different countries in Asia and elsewhere to follow the Chinese developmental model will lead to a different global order.

Of course, all the abovementioned do not mean that we are moving to a "sinicization" of the globe. As already mentioned, the global system will continue to consist of three capitalist subsystems: the neoliberal subsystem that is mainly represented by the United States, the authoritarian Chinese, and the European one that has social-democratic characteristics (see Chapters 2 and 8). In order for humanity to face global risks mentioned earlier, what is required is cooperation between the two superpowers, mediated by a third, large, economic superpower, the EU.[6] If such a cooperation does not prevail, we may see destructions of a biblical type.

To conclude, the United States, at least in the short term, will continue to play the hegemonic role. But Biden's goal to stop China's rise is utopian. Of course, he will be obliged to react when President Xi Jinping follows illegal policies that are against American interests. But he should not continue to interfere in China's internal developments, as he would not like to see Chinese interference in domestic US affairs. President Biden's ideological campaign may contribute to the eruption of a new cold war, which may prove much worse than the previous one.[7] It is for this reason that the EU and the strongest EU powers (Germany, France) must pursue in a more dynamic, resolute manner a strategy of autonomy of the EU. A strategy aiming at moving the world from a destructive confrontation of the two superpowers to cooperation.

Concerning Biden's internal policy, his shift from Trump's neoliberal policies changed to a great extent American society. His plan of construction of a social safety net via an expansion of Medicare, free preschool, community college education, and other measures has reduced the country's rising inequalities.[8] The American president has also supported trade unions. After a decade of decline, unions gained more power and popularity. Of course, there was a corporate reaction via the lobbying process. The National Association of Manufacturers and the US Chamber of Commerce declared their opposition to the government's trade union policy.[9]

Biden has also allocated huge resources aiming at infrastructural modernization. In November 2021 the House of Representatives passed a five-year trillion bill to repair the aging infrastructure of the United States. This achievement was considered similar to Roosevelt's successful attempt to handle the Great Depression.[10] On the other hand, as mentioned earlier, Biden's crusade against China accentuated the confrontation between the two superpowers—particularly when he introduced export restrictions blocking China having access to technology on national security grounds.[11]

The American president tried as well to build alliances of democratic countries against China. He insisted, for instance, that Germany should not continue with an investment agreement between Germany and China. Merkel answered that such projects will strengthen the country's cooperation with China, reducing therefore the present growing confrontation between the two superpowers.

Scholz, the successor to Merkel in the German Chancellery, followed in the steps of his predecessor. He visited China in December 2022, the first European leader to pay such a visit in three years.[12] After all, Germany has strengthened its economic ties with China, as the latter country bought a stake in Germany's largest harbor, Hamburg.

The American president was also opposed to the Russian-Germany Nord Stream 2 project. The chancellor's reply was that the EU must have good relations with both Russia (before the Ukrainian crisis) and China. Macron stressed as well that European and American interests do not always coincide.

Not only Biden's ideological war is counterproductive, it is also based on contradictory principles. For instance, for the American president it is wrong for Western allies to cooperate with authoritarian countries like China and Russia. But it is acceptable to do so with US allies, some of which are equally authoritarian. To be more specific, Biden called Putin a criminal who was behind attempts to kill the Russian opposition's leader Navalny. That was probably a correct assessment, but Biden had effectively ignored Saudi Arabia's prince Mohamed's successful attempt to kill in the cruelest way a dissident journalist, Khashoggi.[13] This type of inconsistencies undermines Biden's ideological project.

Undoubtedly, as already mentioned, Biden's critique of Chinese authoritarianism is correct. But it is obvious that his ideological campaign will not have an impact inside China's authoritarian regime. Instead, it will lead to a growing confrontation that will make very difficult, if not impossible, a cooperation that is a precondition for dealing with global risks.[14]

What aggravated further the abovementioned situation was the agreement signed in September 2021 between Australia, the UK, and the United States (AUKUS) to develop Australian submarines that will have nuclear weapons. Biden's goal was to undermine China's dominance in the Pacific Ocean. But the AUKUS will further deteriorate the relations between the two superpowers.[15] Moreover, it has also damaged relations between the United States and Europe since the latter was not consulted. Particularly France reacted more drastically.

Before the UK-US agreement, the French government had an agreement with Australia to help the modernization of Australia's submarines without the installation of nuclear weapons. The French reaction to the AUKUS agreement was to recall its ambassadors from Australia and the Unites States. As a result of the abovementioned reactions, Biden reinforced Trump's attempt to distantiate the United States from the EU. It is not therefore surprising that the European Commission's president, Ursula von der Leyen, suggested that the EU should accelerate its autonomy policy vis-à-vis the United States and China—this of course before the Ukrainian crisis.

Another point to stress is that the US president's goal to undermine the Chinese dominance in the Pacific is primarily based on weapons. Whereas the Chinese dominance is primarily based on trade. China has important economic relations with many countries in the Pacific region, relations that the countries involved do not want to disrupt.

Finally, the Taliban takeover in Afghanistan, after the Americans left the country in August 2021, undermined Biden's policy abroad. He was right, of course, to continue Trump's policy of ending a twenty-year-long war. But his idea to withdraw American troops abruptly was wrong. The sudden departure, without any consultation with his allies, was disastrous both for the public image of the United States as a superpower and for the segments of Afghani population which considered the Taliban regime illegitimate and had taken sides with the West in its war against the Taliban.[16]

What the US administration, both under Trump and under Biden, may have not fully absorbed is a new world reality. There is a tectonic change that the phenomenal, economic, and geopolitical power of the Chinese giant has brought about. The rapid globalization and China's advance led to a change to the balance of power between "the West and the rest"; a change that we think that it is irreversible. If the United States is building alliances, so does China. The huge Chinese investments of the Silk Road, despite its shortcomings, led several countries in Asia and elsewhere to adopt a developmental model that combines capitalism with an authoritarian political system.

Biden's idea of gradually democratizing China or preventing its further expansion is utopian. This does not mean that he should not interfere when President Xi adopts illegitimate policies that undermine American geopolitical interests. But he must stop interfering with what happens inside China. If changes come, they will occur from within China rather than from the outside, because any foreign interference leads to the growth of Chinese nationalism and the further consolidation of the Chinese regime.

Given the abovementioned discussion, as we will argue in Chapter 5, the American president will have to choose: either he pursues an ideological, political, and geopolitical confrontation with China or he seeks a cooperation that is the precondition for facing global risks. As far as the EU is concerned, as long as capitalism survives, the European social-democratic system remains the only road to a more civilized and humane social order.

We believe that this is recognized by anyone who has observed on the one hand the increasing economic hardship of Americans who are not shielded by a developed welfare state, the polarization of American society between Republicans and Democrats, the culture wars ravaging the American public sphere, and the constraints put on human rights, including recent challenges to women's rights; and on the other hand the increasing control that Xi's regime exerts on the life of Chinese citizens, the suppression of dissidents and of ethnic and religious minorities, the growth of an upper class that leads a life of luxury beyond what the Chinese middle and lower classes could ever imagine, and the corruption that has become endemic among the political and entrepreneurial elites in today's China.

Notes

1 See Pew Research Center (2021).

2 See Kucik (2021).

3 See Vesoulis (2020).

4 See Vartan (2022).

5 See Bledsoe (2023).

6 In Chapter 5 we argue that in addition to the two superpowers (the United States and China), the EU could also play an important role. Hence, we propose the possibility of a tripolar global governance (the United States, China, the EU).

7 At the beginning of 2001, 14 percent of Americans viewed China as an enemy. Later, due to Biden's aggressive foreign policy 45 percent of the population considered the Chinese giant a hostile force.

8 Due to various reactions, Biden's anti-poverty program was attenuated (see *The Economist*, April 2, 2022). But later Biden's reforms were successful. A legislative proposal that became law entails the dedication of huge funds for fighting climate change and for other social measures.

9 See *The Economist*, December 11, 2021.

10 See *The Economist*, November 13, 2021.

11 Biden in a more systematic manner than Trump tried to show and undermine China's rise.

12 See Tao (2022).

13 See Bledsoe (2023).

14 Concerning US-China relations there was a recent conference at Harvard University on "The Future of US–China relations: Competition, Coexistence,

Cooperation." Participants were from both China and the United States. Closing the symposium, the former US ambassador to China said "frankly we should try to communicate, we should try negotiation." We think that one needs communication and also competition and coexistence. That would be legitimate competition in trade and coexistence in the sense that each of the two superpowers should accept the other's existence.

15 See Cohen (2023).

16 See *The Economist*, August 21, 2021.

5

Globalization and Global Governance

While a first phase of economic globalization occurred at the turn of the nineteenth to the twentieth century, the corresponding second phase at the end of the twentieth century was larger in scale and different because it took the form of financialization. In the earlier phase, globalization was propelled by industrialization and colonial expansion. In the later phase, financial capital became more mobile and prevalent. More concretely, the high frequency and large size of capital movements across the world affected many national economies that—comparatively speaking—were less competitive. National borders became porous, within larger economic regions.[1]

The end of the nation-state, however, did not take place. In the EU, most member states remained the principal actors, that is, the protagonists of European integration, while EU-level bodies (e.g., the European Commission) continued to play the role of the agent. Large international players, such as the United States, expanded their national military and technological capabilities, particularly after facing asymmetrical threats from non-state actors (e.g., the Al-Qaeda).

In this chapter we discuss recent transformations of globalization and the rising need for new global governance in a world that is not characterized any more by the preponderant role that the United States played at the turn of the twentieth to the twenty-first century.

After the rise of China, a major debate is whether the United States will continue playing the hegemonic role not only in the West, as in the early postwar period, but globally. For many observers, the United States will continue to be the global hegemon as it did after 1989. In that year, as it is well known, the socialist pole of the bipolar global order collapsed. The system had overstrained itself in decades-long economic and armament competition with the West.

State socialist regimes had also been delegitimized domestically, owing to lack of freedom, stagnation, and the decline of the living standards. Symbolically the fall of state socialism occurred on November 9, 1989, when the East German communist regime gave East Germans access to West Berlin.[2] The Berlin Wall fell and the United States almost overnight became an unassailable economic, military, and diplomatic power in the world. For other observers, given the change in the power balance between the Western developed countries and the rise of China, sooner or later the Chinese giant will occupy the hegemonic throne.

In the geopolitical sphere, according to Joseph Nye, the United States will preserve its leading role.[3] Only an alliance between China and India could lead to the opposite—something not probable at present. Moreover, in terms of technological development and scientific research, the United States seems to prevail. For instance, the more important Chinese exports in high technology are produced by branches of American multinational companies.

Jessica T. Mathews stresses another advantage of the American superpower.[4] The author points out that a hegemonic dominance does not only depend on the economic or geopolitical power. It also depends on cultural orientations and values. After the Second World War, Western values spread globally— values such as the emphasis on individual freedom, political liberalism, and the rule of law. As a result, the global system remains more Western/democratic rather than authoritarian. This is not persuasive. As we explain in Chapter 9, for a variety of reasons, democracies are declining in numbers and autocracies are multiplying. As far as authoritarian China is concerned, its transformation into a democracy, in the short or medium term, is impossible (see Chapter 3). In the very long term, a political opening in China might occur mainly because of internal developments.

As mentioned earlier, in terms of innovation the United States prevails. On the other hand, due to globalization, knowledge in all fields spreads rapidly.[5] Therefore, Chinese attempts to "steal" technologies and scientific knowledge cannot be prevented. Digitalization tends to overcome the monopolization of knowledge (see *The Economist*, March 17, 2018). Moreover, we often observe the "frog leaping" phenomenon. For instance, Ant Financial, a Chinese corporation focusing on automatic digital payments, has developed a new method of payments without bank intermediaries. More generally, the rapid growth of the Chinese economy and the spreading of its model in other countries may lead the Chinese giant becoming the next hegemon.

If none of the two superpowers prevails, is there any other possibility? We think that a third possibility could be a system of global tripolar governance. That is a cooperation/alliance between the three global actors (the United States, China, the EU) based on a type of governance able to deal with risks that cannot be tackled otherwise. More specifically, as the United States during the postwar period set the basic rules in the Western monetary system, something similar could be achieved today at the level of a capitalist system that has prevailed everywhere.

As we have already mentioned in Chapter 2, today there are three capitalist subsystems (the neoliberal whose main representative is the United States, the Chinese authoritarian, and the EU social democratic). They have, of course, different political and cultural systems.

Given this, there is also the view that global cooperation is impossible. For instance, Graham Allison has argued that in the same way that in ancient Greece Sparta challenged the Athenian hegemony leading to a destructive war, something similar could happen between the rising Chinese giant and the declining American one.[6] We think that this thesis (the so-called Thucydides Trap) is wrong. In the social sciences there are no universal theories that ignore *contextualization*. Given that the ancient Greek context is different from the present global one, a theory claiming the inevitability of war between the two superpowers is misleading. The growing interdependence of countries (in terms of trade, scientific developments, the circulation of ideas, etc.) and the realization of world leaders that in a global confrontation there will be no winners may lead to a China-US cooperation.

This is possible because, unlike Trump's dogma of "America first," Biden wants to avoid a catastrophic global war. Given the overall strategy of the present American president, at some point he will realize that his ideological attack on China leads nowhere. If Biden had to choose between global war and cooperation, there is no doubt that he would choose the latter. Unlike Trump's ethnocentric fanaticism, Biden is more realistic. Of course, a type of cooperation between the two superpowers cannot be an *ad hoc* affair. It requires *institutionalized rules and procedures* able to provide the framework within which resources can be mobilized in order to save humanity from global catastrophes.

A way to support the idea of global governance is to look at the globalization process. According to Immanuel Wallerstein,[7] globalization started in the sixteenth century, when in Europe a configuration emerged within which states were competing with each other without one of them becoming dominant, creating thus an *imperium*.[8]

After the collapse of the Soviet Union, capitalism, with few exceptions (e.g., North Korea), continued its expansion, but transnational corporations were not able to penetrate the periphery of the global capitalist system. It is only today that the penetration process has been completed. It is now that a corporation can create branches not only in the capital of a country, but in most of its urban and semi-urban centers. Thus, a product like a Samsung TV can be rapidly acquired almost everywhere.

There is a second dimension of overall globalization; deep penetration has been combined with full communicational interaction.[9] A person today can call instantly friends and relatives in the other end of the planet, often free of charge. It is in that sense that globalization at present has a *unique character*. It is a fully developed "globality." Given the abovementioned discussion, risks as well become global. Pandemics, ecological destruction, and nuclear confrontation between superpowers cannot be limited/localized. For instance, contrary to what happened with the bombing of Japan during the Second World War where the allies were the winners, today there cannot be winners and losers. There can be *only losers*.

Needless to say, globalization was not continuous. During the two world wars of the previous century, walls were raised between opponents. And as we will argue in Chapter 7, the same happened during the pandemic and the Ukrainian crisis. After thirty years of continuous globalization, a process of deglobalization reappeared.[10] Given the problems of supply chains and Russia's threats of stopping completely the provision of gas and oil to the EU and to other countries, there was the adoption of a self-reliance strategy moving from outsourcing to "local sourcing"[11] as well as a strategy to find energy in other parts of the globe.

Despite the abovementioned discussion, *globalization continues*. For example, scientific knowledge and cultural ways of living cannot be stopped by building walls. Moreover, and this is very important, given that global risks like ecological destruction or a nuclear war have effects that spread everywhere, at some point chances are that globalization may return via cooperation between the superpowers. And the way to deal with the abovementioned situation is not only through the mobilization of forces from below (e.g., social movements). One also needs the cooperation of mega-actors who have the capacity to handle effectively global dangers.

Take the example of climate change. Here we observe a constant clash between the developed and the less developed countries. As was shown in the international climate change conferences in 2021 and 2022 (the COP26 and the COP27),[12] developed countries are not prepared to provide adequate funds to the less developed ones. Moreover, formal commitments made at the two conferences, even if realized, cannot solve the growing ecological risks. According to Thomas Piketty, it is impossible to fight seriously climate change without a radical redistribution of wealth and income.[13] However, this is an important statement that rich countries and billionaires do not take into account. As this is a global problem, neither billionaires nor some rich counties can solve it.

We think only a cooperation between a tripolar global governance between the United States, China, and the EU can effectively deal with this problem. Of course, several left-wing analysts argue that within capitalism the reduction of inequalities is not possible. But we think that, given that the capitalist mode of production will still survive for a very long time (see Chapter 1), without a global governance like the one we are proposing, irreversible ecological destruction will unavoidably occur. Piketty is right about the need for a radical redistribution of wealth. But he does not tell us how to reduce global inequalities before it is too late. Take, for instance, the project of decarbonization, which requires huge resources. This is a project that at present moves so slowly that an overall ecological catastrophe is a reasonable possibility.[14]

Instead of a bipolar, is a tripolar global governance possible? If one takes into account that the global capitalist system entails three subsystems whose major representatives, as already mentioned, are the United States, China, and the EU, we think it is possible. Of course, one can argue that the EU is not a superpower because, despite its economic and political power, its military forces are very limited. But the EU, given its history, its civilizing/humanistic traditions, and the fact that it promotes the spread of civic, political, and social rights downward in society, can become an arbitrator between the two superpowers.

During the face-to-face meetings between Biden and Xi, both presidents declared that they want the end of the Ukrainian war, and they also foresee collaboration in areas of common interests like climate change[15] and the avoidance of a nuclear war.[16] There is no reason not to believe them. There are of course differences, like the Taiwan question or more generally geopolitical competition. But in so far as global power leaders do not want a nuclear war, the condition for a global tripolar governance is possible. Or to put it differently, a global tripolar alliance between the United States, China, and the EU, in cooperation with other international organizations and the billions of people who want a more humane global order from below, is the only way forward.

In a fully globalized planet, global governance must be different. If one takes into account the existence of the Chinese authoritarian giant, the idea of a global democracy is utopian. More pessimist analysts predict the emergence of a Chinese hegemony imposing a global authoritarian framework. We think both ideas are not convincing.[17]

We think that what is unique at present is that, given the rise of China, the United States cannot establish a very strong hegemony as the one achieved in the second half of the twentieth century. The reason is that at that time the United States managed to prevail over the defeated Nazi Germany, the authoritarian Japan and later the collapse of the Soviet Union. Today it cannot defeat the Chinese giant. Therefore, cooperation rather than confrontation is possible. Taking into account the abovementioned discussion, we argue that an institutionalized tripolar governance can establish a relatively stable global order.

For some observers, the abovementioned idea sounds like a dictatorial solution in a multipolar world. But for the same reason that after the early postwar period the American government, despite its hegemony, could not impose by force its will on all Western states, the same can be possible for a global tripolar governance that could create an overall framework within which one can provide incentives as well as sanctions to those (e.g., ethnocentric governments, anti-green corporations) that ignore global risks.

There are other theoretical attempts that propose a type of global democratization that could render hegemons not necessary. David Held has worked out a complex framework for a democratic, cosmopolitan governance.[18] Given the number of countries, the variety of cultures, and political regimes, his scheme is obviously utopian. A different approach focuses on the need to radically restructure the UN in a way that could replace the need for a global governance.[19] However, the UN, even if restructured, cannot play such a role. The American hegemony was obviously linked with the UN, but the latter did not and could not replace the former.

A theory that is very relevant with the abovementioned arguments is the so-called *Regime Theory* or *International Regime Theory*.[20] Contrary to the realist theory in international relations which argues that conflicts between states prevail and shape the structure of the international system, regime theory points out that there are areas where cooperation rather than conflict exists. These are "regimes" characterized by prevailing norms, rules, and procedures that are compatible with the expectations of actors in a related specific "issue-area." For instance, global trade is such a regime. There are rules and procedures accepted and followed by states that have different political and economic interests. Despite such differences, not all but many governments accept such rules, because they lead to growth and prosperity for the participants.

Problems like pandemics or climate change can be dealt on three levels— the micro, the meso, and the macro.

On the micro-level, many serious studies have shown how risks like the Covid-19 or climate change can be tackled by specifying clearly goals and means to achieve them—means such as constant measuring of results, collaboration between government, business, and civil society, provision of reliable information to the large public about failures or achievements, and the like.[21]

On the meso-level, we think positively about collective actors that operate in today's multipolar world. These are collective actors like the G7 or organizations like the World Bank or the IMF which try to help semi-peripheral or very poor countries to develop. We also positively consider events leading to international agreements on climate change like those of Paris, Glasgow, and Sharm-El-Sheikh—agreements that aim to fight ecological destruction.

However, we think that less attention is given on the *macro-level*. On how superpowers like the United States and China have tried, but on the whole have failed to contribute to the solution of problems related to climate change, to disarmament, and to the possibilities of a catastrophic third world war.

In this chapter, we have already argued that despite periods of deglobalization, at present the world is moving to "full" globalization. This is a globalization in which risks, when realized, have catastrophic effects not only on parts of the globe but on the whole planet. Therefore, the goal on this level is to link the micro- and meso-levels to a macro-institutionalized framework within which mega-actors can provide resources (economic, political, and cultural) in order to avoid overall catastrophes and achieve a planetwide survival. More specifically, the framework would be an arrangement of tripolar global governance (the United States-China-the EU). In our view, it is not possible to deal with global risks without moving from the meso-level to the macro-level. In other words, a global tripolar hegemony cannot be ignored or underemphasized. If it is, there can be no convincing proposal of how to save the world. Macro-actors' cooperation is a *precondition*.

As already mentioned, in a fully globalized world leaders have only one choice. Either to accept a win-win game that brings profits to all or a lose-lose game that leads to overall destruction. Cooperation in the form of global institutionalized governance is the only rational solution for tackling global risks. But historical developments have rarely followed a course based on reason. Can rationality prevail today? Maybe, since today we face a *unique* situation. A situation in which most world leaders realize there is no other survival solution.

When this happens, the question is how global stability can come about. It would be a stability that is one of the main preconditions for handling global risks. There are two obstacles that at present prevent it: Biden's crusade against China and Putin's revisionist strategy aiming at the restoration of another Russian empire. Concerning the United States, the American president will eventually realize the impossibility of preventing the further Chinese development. He will also realize that the rise of China is not reversible. Biden will have to accept that as long as capitalism survives, there will be neither a global democratization nor a victory of democracy over autocracy. The existence of the two worlds is unavoidable. A precondition for global peace.

As to the Russian obstacle, here China can help constrain Russia. Putin may have formidable nuclear weapons, but at present he desperately needs China's political and financial support. As is well known, the Chinese president does not want to stop the profitable trade and investment relations he has with the EU. More generally he wants a global stability that helps China to continue its economic growth. At some point Xi Jinping will persuade or force Putin to forget his revisionist dreams and turn his attention to the latter's continuous miscalculations, pointing out that it would be better to forget Russia's nuclear threats and try to revive Russia's impoverished economy.

If the above two obstacles are eliminated, if Biden stops his ideological war against China, and if Putin forgets his phantasy of rebuilding a Russian empire, there will be a possibility for a US-China cooperation and even for the establishment of a tripolar, institutionalized governance between the United States, China, and the EU.[22]

Multipolarity

In this section we will argue that the idea of coordinating various poles, states, networks, and groups like G7 or G20 cannot establish a global order, that is, an order capable to deal with global risks. Such coordination attempts invariably lead to a type of *fragmentation* that, as we will argue later, leads not to order but to global disorder. In the following we will give some examples of theories which do not deal adequately with the issue of global governance.

Hierarchies, Markets, Networks

The idea that governance in the contemporary world does not need to follow Weber's ideal type of bureaucracy has been suggested by economists and sociologists analyzing organizations in the private sector. For example, in 1983 Oliver E. Williamson suggested that markets and hierarchies are two distinct organizational forms bearing different transaction costs.[23] Further on, sociologists, such as Manuel Castells, have discussed networks as forms of social organization at the level of national societies.[24] Michael Mann has put historical depth to the analysis of societies as sets of networks.[25] Similar ideas have been transplanted to the study of global governance, to which we now turn.

We will start with an important work entitled *Global Governance in a World of Change*, edited by Michael N. Barnett, Jon C. W. Pevenhouse, and Kal Raustiala.[26] All contributors accept a basic framework that consists of three models of governance: hierarchies, networks, and markets. They argue that after the Second World War, hierarchies became less important than markets and networks. Given this they attempt to explore if such changes lead to more or less effective results in a variety of "issue areas." But this type of conceptualization does not lead to an overall analysis of global governance. It leads to a myriad of fragments which cannot help dealing with today's global risks that, as we have already mentioned, are mainly irreversible ecological destruction and the possibility of a third world war nuclear catastrophe.

It is interesting at this point to refer to the UN secretary-general, Antonio Guterres. In an address in 2019 he pointed out that whereas the global challenges are more and more *integrated*, responses are more *fragmented*. "If this is not reversed, it is a recipe for disaster."[27] The way we have interpreted the earlier discussion is that today challenges/global risks, like ecological destruction and global nuclear war, are *integrated*, whereas responses are fragmented, that is, entirely inadequate. From this point of view, multipolarity has no solution of what matters more at present. It does not tell us how we can move from fragmentation to an effective handling of the two abovementioned major risks. This does not mean that authors contributing to the aforementioned volume do not provide useful insights into a variety of issues. But definitely they tell us very little about *global* governance in a changing world.

Institutions and Social Change

In his book, *How Global Institutions Rule the World*, Josep M. Colomer provides interesting information—from the categorization of global groups referring to "network groups, competitive global groups, conflicting global groups" to the idea of "accountable democracy."[28] But despite its merits, his overall argument has a weak theoretical basis when he argues that institutions "rule the world." The emphasis on institutions is misleading. Institutions are reified in his analysis. They are transformed into anthropomorphic entities that can change the world. For it is only when institutions are *dialectically articulated with actors* that order or disorder can be explained. Of course, the author mentions groups/actors but he assigns them a peripheral role. Like the well-known American theorist Talcott Parsons,[29] Colomer shows how institutions have an impact on actors but not the other way around. Collective actors operating within an institutional setting are portrayed as passive products of institutional contradictions.[30]

Beyond Multipolarity

Dani Rodrik and Stephen Walt have suggested a path to reconstruct world order.[31] Although, Rodrik and Walt refer to a bipolarity or a highly uneven multipolarity, basically their focus is on the former. They argue that the future of a global order will depend to a considerable extent on the state of relations between the United States and China. Their position comes near to our proposal that a tripolar global arrangement (US-China-EU) would be the only way to move to a state where present global risks can be dealt with.

To conclude, in this chapter, we have emphasized that only such a solution can provide an *institutionalized* framework able to provide the resources (economic, political, social, geopolitical) for the survival of the planet.

Notes

1 For a summary of alternative approaches to globalization, see Lemert et al. (2010).
2 See Garton Ash (1999).
3 See Nye (2005 and 2015).
4 See Mathews (2017).
5 See Romer (1990, 1994).
6 See Allison (2017).
7 See Wallerstein (1974).
8 From Wallerstein's theory onward when reference is made to globalization, the focus is on the economic sphere, namely on the expansion of markets, supply chains, and multinational corporations penetrating the periphery. In this context, one also refers to periods during which walls are raised and the world moves to economic deglobalization, for instance, during the First and the Second World Wars. *But there are other types of globalization* which do not follow this economic pattern. This is obvious in the sociocultural and scientific spheres.

Sociocultural globalization refers, for instance, to consumption patterns or individualistic modes of living that spread gradually to urban centers worldwide. To give a specific example, the Ukrainian crisis led to the restriction of capital movements from the Western powers to Russia and vice versa. But this partial economic deglobalization did not prevent the continuation of an individualistic style of living in Russia's urban centers and elsewhere. Something similar one observes in the development of scientific knowledge. Here deglobalization is different or impossible. A good example is the spreading of specialized knowledge leading to the production of nuclear weapons. A production that we observe in several of countries. Trade wars can lead to deglobalization but geopolitical wars do not. More generally, scientific knowledge may lead not only to destruction but also to medical advances (e.g., the fight against cancer) that cannot be stopped. No country, however powerful, can monopolize scientific advances. To conclude, economic deglobalization cannot today prevent the gradual, continuous globalization of sociocultural patterns and scientific advances.

9   Full communication interaction is also relevant, as far as work is concerned. Workers may be unable to move physically. But remote-control technologies can solve the problem (see *The Economist*, February 18, 2023).

10 See Goldberg and Reed (2023).

11 Because of the Ukrainian crisis, safety prevailed over efficiency. According to the *Economist* (June 18, 2022) switching to a "security-first" model of development will lead to insularity and stagnation. But we think there should be more balance between security and efficiency—the latter leading to growth.

12 International conferences to manage the climate change took place in 2021 in Glasgow (the COP26) and in 2022 in Sharm-El-Sheikh (the COP27). States, NGOs, and international organizations participated in the conferences.

13 See Piketty (2022).

14 Decarbonization is not only difficult in the United States and China, it is more so in the developing countries (*The Economist*, January 1, 2022).

15 Antonio Guterres (secretary-general of the UN) declared that as far as climate is concerned, we will have "either climate solidarity pact or collective suicide." Finally in Egypt in November 2022 (at the COP27) there was an agreement to create a fund to pay for climate-related damage in poorer countries (the so-called Sharm el-Sheikh Implementation Plan). But there was no agreement on greater cuts to greenhouse gas emissions and to end fossil fuel use.

16 Pelosi's visit to Taiwan led to a termination of collaboration between the United States and China. But after the face-to-face relations between the two presidents in Bali, on November 14, 2022, there was an agreement to restart collaboration in areas of common interests.

17 They are not convincing because the Americanization or sinicization of the world is inconceivable. If not for any other reason, because before the overall dominance of one superpower prevails, there will be a nuclear war. Something that neither Biden nor Xi Jinping want.

18 See Held (1995 and 2017).

19 See Colomer and Beale (2020).

20 See Hasenclever, Mayer, and Rittberger (1997).

21 Mazzucato's well-known work (2013) is a very good example of this type of approach. See also Doerr (2018).

22 If this happens there will certainly be global growth and global prosperity. Inequalities will also grow, but a tripolar governance can more effectively reduce them.

23 See Williamson (1983).

24 See Castells (2010).

25 See Mann (1986, 1993).

26 See Barnett, Pevenhouse, and Raustiala (2022).

27 The quotation is mentioned in an article by Orfeo Fioretos included in *Global Governance in a World of Change*, p. 340.

28 See Colomer (2014).

29 See Parsons (1951).

30 The extreme multipolarity is developed by Roberto Unger (2022) who argues that one can govern the world without any type of world governance. Another form of multipolarity is the idea of collaboration of countries, both democratic and authoritarian, which want to establish a stable global order. In this case as well there is no attempt to show how these stability loving countries will be coordinated.

31 See Rodrik and Walt (2021).

Part 3

From the National to the Post-National Level

6

The Golden Years—Social Democracy (1945–75)

The Second International, founded in 1889, was explicitly Marxist. For example, the German Social Democratic Party that was founded in 1875 was a revolutionary organization. Its aim was to emancipate the workers and establish a communist society. The same was true about Lenin's revolutionary Russian Social Democratic Party.[1]

It is in the early twentieth century that we observe the division between revolutionary and reformist parties—the latter adopting an evolutionist orientation toward progress. Kautsky tried to bring together the two approaches. He argued that revolution is not the only way to promote workers' interests.[2]

The definitive break between revolutionary and reformist social democratic parties occurred when social democrats rejected or transformed radically Marx's work and accepted key ministerial roles.[3] This was the position of the French socialist Jean Jaurès and Eduard Bernstein. The latter, even before the Second World War, argued that the improvement of the workers' situation via democratic parliamentary means is a basic precondition for the transcendence of capitalism and the passage to *democratic socialism*, that is a post-capitalist situation where the control of the means of production will be mainly based on cooperative values and practices. Finally, Bernstein's strategy prevailed, and this led to social democracy's thirty "golden years" (1945–75).

During this period, social democratic parties in Europe were often in government and diffused civic, political, and social rights to the base of the social pyramid. They strengthened the rule of law, gave to all adult citizens the right to vote, and developed in an unprecedented manner the welfare state.[4] It was an achievement never seen before in the history of capitalism.

Concerning the spread of rights downward in society, an interesting point is the emphasis given on the right of nondiscrimination based on inequalities in terms of ability/inability, age, ethnicity, race, religion, sexual orientation, and cultural identities. Another important dimension, which led to an overall more peaceful social situation, was the corporatist system of decision-making in the economic sphere. There was in North and Central European countries a tripartite collaboration between capital, labor, and the government.[5]

Given the abovementioned discussion, it is not surprising that the UN World Happiness Report argued that the "happy" nations are mainly social democratic. They are characterized by public and general welfare services, high life expectancy, civil liberties, a free press, and lower inequalities.

As we will explain more extensively in Chapter 7, it was mainly the opening of the world markets in the late 1970s which led to a situation where capital was not any more restrained by state regulations or trade unions' demands for higher wages and better work conditions. Whenever capital was facing such problems, it could move to countries where trade unions were weak and governments more market oriented.

Given the abovementioned conditions, social democratic parties had to broaden their working-class base and appeal to the middle classes–becoming thus "catch all parties," in order to survive. They also had to adopt quasi-neoliberal practices and values, encapsulated in the quasi-neoliberal "Washington Consensus." Finally, the 2008–9 economic crisis (see Chapter 7) created doubts about this consensus.

After 2010 there were mass protests against austerity policies in countries of the European periphery.

An interesting analysis of the historical development of human rights is provided by the well-known social scientist T. H. Marshall.[6] According to him the movement for the expansion of rights started in the seventeenth century. During this period, given that social institutions (family, labor market, etc.) were not differentiated, rights were also not differentiated. It was only during the eighteenth and nineteenth centuries that we observe a distinction between political and social rights.

First, rights referring to property, freedom of speech, and freedom of religious beliefs and practices were developed. These rights undermined the feudal principle of social stratification. They gradually established the idea of the rule of law. It is therefore in the sphere of law and in courts that we observe the first transition from a situation where different legal codes and procedures were applied to different classes to a situation in which all citizens were equal under the law. The second major step was the graduate abolition of restrictions concerning the right to vote and to be elected in parliament.

Finally, the third major advance was the construction of a unified civic community which occurred in twentieth century with the development of social rights—the right of everyone to a decent education, to health care, and to social transfers and social care for old age. During this phase the institutional focus shifted again, this time from the political to the social sphere, as reflected in the massive development of schools, hospitals, health care, and community centers, among numerous other welfare services.

The introduction of social rights is a move, however hesitant, from formal to substantive equality, from class inequalities to relative citizenship equality. While class differences easily undermine equality, the spread of social rights gives greater substance and meaning to citizens' civil and political rights. It ensures that people's legal and political participation in the community is not a mere formality.

This does not mean that the development of the social aspects of citizenship eliminates class inequalities. What it does mean is that in capitalist conditions citizenship rights can never eliminate class inequalities, but they can certainly mitigate their worst excesses.

Marshall's analysis written in the mid-twentieth century did not include cultural rights or gender rights that are of great significance today. In so far as Marshall's account *describes* the broad macro-stages in the construction of the modern citizenship community, what are the basic mechanisms that explain such a transformation? Here Marshall's texts are less informative. Clearly his overall aim was to provide a detailed description rather than an explanation of the transformation. But in so far as he briefly refers to transformative mechanisms, he understood them from the point of view of agency rather than of the social system.

To use Lockwood's well-known distinction, Marshall was focusing on social-integration rather than system-integration perspective.[7] The spread of rights has more to do with collective *actors* and their struggles, and less with *systemic* requirements leading to differentiation and greater adaptive capacity.

Marshall points out, for instance, that the social aspects of citizenship would not have been possible without the prior acquisition of political rights that enabled the working classes to organize themselves politically. Moreover, it was only when the civil liberties of free speech and the right to form associations were exercised collectively (via the creation of large trade unions) that the welfare state became a possibility.

Needless to say, Marshall's analysis, based as it was on long-term historical developments primarily in the UK, cannot be applied in other countries. Even in the case of the UK there were steps forward and steps backward. But as a general overview of the development of rights, Marshall's work is a useful guide for the study of citizenship.

The father of modern sociological theory and well-known American sociologist, Talcott Parsons, used Marshall's insights for his theory of citizenship.[8] He placed them within a broader evolutionary and comparative perspective. In Marshall's analysis the theory of social differentiation is neither explicit, nor does it have any strong explanatory function. In Parsons's analysis, on the other hand, the neo-evolutionist framework on social differentiation takes center stage. This framework allows him both to describe in a theoretically more sophisticated manner the long-term development of citizenship in modern societies and to explain this from a systemic, functionalist (but non-teleological) perspective.

For Parsons, the first major breakthrough in the transition from early to late modernity came with the English Industrial Revolution. This great upheaval led to the constitution of an *economic* subsystem, which, for Parsons, is clearly separate from the three other major societal subsystems: the *political*/goal achievement, the *social*/integration, and the *cultural*/latency subsystem. The great transformation, by dramatically freeing land, capital, and labor from ascriptive controls, by allowing these three "factors of production" to follow a strictly market logic, very quickly established an economic space quite distinct from that of the other three subsystems. It is in this differentiated space that the American theorist locates Marshall's idea about the development of civil rights. It is civil rights related to property, to contractual relations between labor and capital, and to the freedom of all to sell their labor power as a commodity, which established everyone's equality, not only under the law, but also in the marketplace.

The second major breakthrough in the long-term process of differentiation came with the French Revolution. This brought the distinct emergence of a national societal community (Parsons's integration subsystem) that includes all members of society, not any longer on a particularistic but on a universalistic basis. In this new context, therefore, the emphasis was less on economic freedom and more on political equality. This found expression in the French Declaration of the Rights of Man. It is here that citizenship becomes the central concept of "the claim of the whole population on inclusion," on the basis of one-man, one-vote. Moreover, members of society were to be considered not only free and equal, but also bound together in a national autonomous community.

This type of democratic revolution led to the transition from a particularistic solidarity of the premodern communities (based as it was on ethnicity, language, religion, etc.) to a universalistically defined solidarity leading to a non-fragmented, nationally unitary modern community. In this way, Marshall's idea of the development of political rights in the UK is generalized and placed by Parsons in a conceptual framework that focuses on the differentiation of early modern societies into the four subsystems of the social system mentioned earlier.

Finally, if the first differentiation breakthrough came in England and the second in France, the third occurred in the other side of the Atlantic. In the United States, according to Parsons, the development of civil and political rights was complemented, however rudimentarily, with the expansion of education. It is in that country that a third revolution took place: the educational one that, in its consequences, was to be as crucial as its industrial and democratic predecessors.

Prior to the educational revolution, access to education in the United States was limited to a small elite. The mass of the population remained illiterate. For Parsons, the

> attempt to educate the whole population was a radical departure. ... This movement has thus meant an immense extension of equality of opportunity ...
> The relatively stable situation of late nineteenth-century Europe accorded higher education to a small elite group, never more than 5 percent of the age group. The United States has broken decisively with this limitation; the proportion of youth receiving some higher education is around 40 percent and is steadily edging upward.[9]

The educational revolution brought with it a radical differentiation between the societal community and the cultural or latency or pattern-maintenance subsystem. As is well known, Parsons's latency subsystem is concerned both with the institutionalization and maintenance of society's core values, as well as with the strengthening of people's motivational commitments to such values. The educational revolution, by contributing significantly to both of these functional requirements, enabled the cultural/latency subsystem to become relatively autonomous from the societal community.

Based on the abovementioned theoretical insights from twentieth-century social democracy, we think that social democratic ideas, uploaded on to the supranational stage, can be very useful in the twenty-first century for a new global arrangement to prevent global risks. As long as capitalism does not collapse, social democracy is the only capitalism with a human face. Social democracy cannot transform the world. But it can help the two superpowers (China and the United States) to move from the present growing confrontation to cooperation. Cooperation being the only way to cope effectively with global risks. Therefore, fighting for social democracy gives meaning to those who hope for a safer and better social world.

To conclude, social democracy's peak of political influence in the years 1945–75 was closely associated with the expansion and differentiation of human rights in the different subsystems of society under postwar capitalism.

Notes

1   See Moschonas (2002).
2   See Sassoon (1996).
3   See Przeworski (1985).
4   See Esping-Andersen (1990).
5   See Schmitter (1974).
6   See Marhsall (1964).
7   See Lockwood (1964).
8   See Parsons (1951).
9   Ibid., 95.

Five Crises: Economic, Pandemic, Ukrainian, Taiwan, and Energy

The subsystems of society, in which social democracy flourished, particularly in North and Western Europe after 1945, were in turn shaped by social democracy. All this changed dramatically in the last quarter of the twentieth century. Social democratic parties faced severe crises, the more recent of which challenged other parties and political systems too and are discussed in the following.

First, post-Fordist industrialization reduced the number of industrial workers.[1] This weakened social democracy's industrial base. It was mainly for this reason that social democratic parties were transformed into "catch-all" political organizations. Another even more important reason for the crisis was the opening of the world markets in the late 1970s. As it is already mentioned, this meant that enterprises had the freedom to transcend national boundaries. They could now easily move to countries where taxation was low and social legislation weak or nonexistent. In order to survive and save some of their past achievements, social democratic governments had to abandon their previous Keynesian policies that at that point were leading to stagflation. To some extent, social democrats were forced to adopt neoliberal values and practices.

For some social democrats, the turn to a neoliberal orientation was an abandonment of social democratic values. It had less to do with necessity and more with wrong strategies. For them the post–golden age social democratic parties are not anymore social democratic. Social democracy does not exist anymore. It is not therefore surprising that radical left parties today reject the social democratic appellation. For other social democrats, however, social democracy's turn was less based on wrong strategies and more to realism—to the realization that due to globalization a return to the past is not possible.[2]

The only way to reduce inequalities and defend a developed welfare state is on a *post-national level*, particularly in the context of the eurozone.

Moving from the crisis of the 1970s to the 2008–9 one, the latter took a global character—in the sense that in terms of its negative effects it resembled the Great Depression of the 1930s. The recent crisis was initially owed to the banks' excessive risk-taking and to the American housing bubble and the eventual bankruptcy of the Lehman Brothers Company. The abovementioned combination led to a global financial crisis resulting in widespread recession, increasing inequalities and massive unemployment and poverty (the "Great Recession").[3]

Concerning the more specific eurozone crisis, which took place after 2009, several EU member states, particularly in the South, were unable to deal with their growing debt without assistance from the European Central Bank (ECB) and the IMF. This situation was aggravated since, due to the common currency (the euro), countries with huge debt were unable to devalue. In 2010 we see the creation of the European Financial Stability Facility. Together with the ECB they provided cheap loans in order to support the main European banks. At the same time there were serious attempts at stricter banking regulation. All of these alleviated some of the problems but, as in the rest of the world, poverty, unemployment, and inequalities were accentuated. Given this, the ECB announced support to members involved in sovereign state bailouts. For instance, Ireland, Portugal, and Greece received EU-IMF bailouts. Later rescue packages were given to Spain and Cyprus.[4]

There is no doubt that these measures attenuated the differences between more and less developed EU countries and enhanced to some extent the socioeconomic integration of the EU. Unfortunately, as the crisis was ending, there was a return to an austerity policy that weakened the positive results of the previous measures.

In the early months of 2020, the Covid-19 pandemic crisis hit the world. Different vaccines against the Covid-19 were produced by pharmaceutical companies. Concerning the vaccination, the European Commission tried but partly failed to implement a common plan. Due to a slow decision-making process, as well as to the failure of companies like AstraZeneca to deliver on time the number of vaccines promised, EU member states pursued national policies. There was "vaccine nationalism," as some countries hoarded vaccines refusing to help other countries within or outside the union. This situation was improved later.

Another negative aspect was that pharmaceutical companies managed to protect their intellectual property rights. They objected to the right of outsiders to produce their vaccines. Pharmaceutical companies argued that that they had dedicated their own private resources to crucial research that led to the rapid production of vaccines. Therefore, it was legitimate to refuse the waiver of their property rights. It was via such monopoly-prone arguments and practices that the companies made colossal profits, while the process of vaccine production was slow. For instance, main pharmaceutical firms produced vaccines covering a very small part of the global population. Given this, those people who were not vaccinated (mainly in the poor countries) could at some point affect those already vaccinated.

The G7 summit in June 2021, which included Germany and France, failed to confront seriously the need for a global solution to the vaccination problem. The measures adopted fell short of meeting the needs of low-income countries. To effectively end the pandemic crisis required the vaccination of 70 percent of the global population, but this goal was ignored by the G7. The IMF's managing director Kristalina Georgieva argued that having the world split into two parts not only does not solve the vaccination problem, but also undermines global economic growth.

President Biden decided to waiver the pharmaceuticals' intellectual property rights. Unfortunately, the EU did not follow the American president's policy. Its leadership (particularly Chancellor Merkel) argued that the waiver was not a solution; if adopted, it would discourage further innovation. According to her, there were more effective ways to help poor counties to deal with Covid-19 disaster. Of course, there were reactions to the abovementioned negative attitude. For this reason, the European Commission president Ursula von der Leyen, although not committed to change the union's policy, said that the matter should be reconsidered. Needless to say, the European support of the pharmaceutical interests had serious consequences for the poor countries whose population was deprived of the means to deal effectively with their tragic situation.

If the rise of China brought a tectonic rift in between the West and the rest (Chapter 3), Russia's Ukrainian invasion in February 2022 had a different but equally profound effect. The invasion was unacceptable. It breached international law and caused innumerable casualties and massive destruction in Ukraine. Moreover, it accentuated antagonisms between the transatlantic block and the Chinese-Russian one. It led to a situation of widespread famine to millions of people in poor countries,[5] as well as serious problems to middle-class families in Europe and elsewhere which could not cope with soaring energy bills. Supply chains were disrupted and the type of deglobalization that we observed during the pandemic was accentuated. Finally, there was the decision of Finland and Sweden to join NATO, despite Turkey's objections.

Of course, after the collapse of the Soviet Union, NATO's expansion justified to some extent the Russian reactions.[6] At present (autumn 2023), however, the situation is different. The Russian president may install more nuclear weapons near the borders of the two Scandinavian countries. Eventually the same will happen on the other side of the borders. Such moves will bring about an unstable balance of power, quite similar to that between the Soviet Union and the United States during the Cuban crisis. Today, of course, there is more geopolitical proximity between the two camps. But we think that the chances of a nuclear confrontation on this issue are rather small.

Due to the Ukrainian crisis, a popular view on global politics today focuses on the consolidation of the two antagonistic blocks. The transatlantic democratic, on the one hand, and the Chinese and its allies, on the other. We think that this dichotomic approach is misleading. For there are many interconnections between the two blocks which have attenuated the confrontational tendencies between the blocks.

To start with, Macron's "autonomy strategy" stresses the need for the EU to follow neither the American nor the Chinese developmental trajectory. Most EU countries, despite Biden's opposition, do not want to break their commercial and political relations with China. And the latter, despite the support it provides to Putin, does not want to break the profitable relationships it has woven with the eurozone.

Of course, the Chinese president is pleased with his alliance with Russia. But, certainly, he does not support Putin's dreams about the creation of a Soviet type Russian empire. President Xi not only wants cooperation with the EU, but also supports global political stability, which is necessary for China's further economic growth. China would not benefit from a military confrontation with the United States and its allies.[7] Another factor to be taken into account is that many countries do not want to take sides by supporting one of the two blocks. This is the case of several African countries as well as India[8] that refuses to condemn Russia's invasion to Ukraine. In fact, none of the member states of the BRICS initiative (Brazil, Russia, India, China, South Africa) condemned that invasion either, as the results of the BRICS summit in August 2023 in Johannesburg showed.

Finally, what is most important is that people all over the planet realize that the continuing confrontation between the United States and China could lead to catastrophic results, like the near-global famine that the Ukrainian war has brought about. Therefore, except for those who still believe that democracy should continue to fight autocracy whatever the consequences, most people around the world would be cautious. They would realize that any aggressive push to effect democratization from abroad, which is compatible with Biden's ideological crusade against China (see Chapter 4), would lead to an impasse. It would lead to a situation where global risks could not be handled effectively. Such a situation may, for instance, be an irreversible ecological destruction affecting particularly poor countries or a new cold world leading to a third world war. To repeat, most people realize that the democracy-autocracy division must be superseded by a new emerging division by those who opportunistically accept the present status quo ("business as usual") and those who realize that cooperation between the two blocks is the basic *precondition* for the planet's survival.

At the time of writing (late summer 2023), after the extraordinary and successful fight of the Ukrainian patriots against the invading Russian forces, it seems that the war will go on longer. Putin's hopes for a rapid takeover were not realized. Ukraine's president Zelensky insists that the fight should continue till his country's territories taken by the Russians are given back. This is a demand Putin will reject, bringing thus the negotiations to an impasse.

As far as the Western alliance is concerned, at the beginning not only the United States, but also all members of the EU condemned Russia's invasion. Later, however, the situation started to change. Several EU member states were reluctant to continue the further sanctions[9] that had to be imposed on Russia, since this will create difficulties to countries that depend in a more direct manner on Russian gas and oil.[10] Even the United States, which provides the bulk of sophisticated weaponry to the Ukrainians, did not want a prolongation of the war, at least initially.[11]

And others went further. Henry Kissinger, for instance, pointed out that the war should not be seen as a punishment or humiliation of Russia.[12] Finally, there is the more general view that one should not prolong a war that reinforces the division between the transatlantic camp and the China-Russia camp, a division that renders impossible the creation of a stable and peaceful situation that most people want.

Putin's invasion of Ukraine and his dreams about the creation of a Soviet type of Russian empire has led many people to forget that it is not only Russia but, to a lesser extent, Western powers that were partly responsible for the present crisis. This is obvious if one takes into account NATO's threat of expansion and the establishment of nuclear weapons in Russia's backyard. As well as Biden's continuing ideological war against China and the by-now forgotten decision of President Bush, in the early 1990s, not to accept the inclusion of Russia into the architecture of a post–Cold War peaceful arrangement.

And, of course, we must not forget that Gorbachev asked Helmut Kohl and the United States, as a condition for his consent of Germany's unification, that NATO does not expand eastward. This was ignored and was a fatal mistake.

Without justifying Putin's violent aggression, it is worth mentioning here that there are non-authoritarian, Western academics who have argued that the main responsibility for the Ukrainian war lies with the West. For instance, John Mearsheimer argued that the war in Ukraine was West's fault, since the United States promised to bring the country into NATO. Moreover, George Kennan described NATO's expansion eastward "as the most fateful error of American policy is the post-cold war era." Of course, there were reactions to the abovementioned criticisms. After all, it was Russia that started and continued a war on Ukraine, hitting civilian targets, in addition to military ones.

As we have already argued, global risks, like irreversible ecological destruction or the possibility of a third world war, can only be avoided if the "democracy versus autocracy" divide is superseded. After the Second World War, the balance of power between the Soviet Union and the United States brought global peace for many years. The same could happen at present. The balance of nuclear power between NATO and Putin's Russia, despite the latter's revisionist phantasies, at least in the short term, cannot bring cooperation, but perhaps a more limited type of confrontation between the superpowers.

Thinking about the possible end of the war, Europeans and Americans declared initially that it is up to the Ukrainians to decide when to stop fighting. President Zelensky in Davos stressed, "Give us weapons and we will get back what is ours." However, Americans started to change their minds. At the beginning, some radical Republicans argued that the United States should stop giving aid to Ukraine. In their view, the huge number of resources, handed out to Ukraine, should rather go to green development[13] or to the modernization of the American fleet in the Pacific Ocean.

Later it was argued that at some point American interests should start diverging from those of Ukraine. The abovementioned position was reinforced by the view that a continuation of a long war could lead to a direct conflict between Russia and NATO, in which case, the possibility of Putin using nuclear weapons cannot be excluded. Finally, a Pew Poll[14] showed that Americans wanted a termination of the war and the start of serious negotiations. This becomes more and more obvious given that neither Putin nor Zelensky can achieve full victory. It is only via negotiations that one can avoid further disasters. In brief, the United States has an interest to press Zelensky to negotiate with Putin. The other great power who can help in this direction is China[15]—given that Putin needs desperately Chinese support.

However, in late 2023, one year after the start of the war, neither Ukraine nor Russia were prepared to negotiate. The latter demanded that Ukraine will not attempt to join NATO and that the Ukrainian government accepts neutrality, moves to demilitarization, and accepts the autonomy of the two parts where Russians are living.[16] Ukraine rejected Putin's terms demanding the return of the country to its prewar frontiers. Obviously, an agreement on the abovementioned terms was not possible. Of course, the terms of that attempted negotiation changed abruptly when China declared that she intends to give lethal arms to Russia. Biden reacted in a very aggressive manner. In February 2023, during his surprise visit to Ukraine, Biden declared that he will do whatever necessary to help the Ukrainians to defeat Russia. This turnout of events means that the situation in Ukraine is aggravated to the extent that perhaps a nuclear confrontation may be possible.

More specifically, regarding the Ukrainian crisis, the plans of the major powers have changed over time. We think that the following changes will occur. *First*, Putin will decide the continuation of the war, the mobilization and militarization of his society, and the further strengthening of his alliance with China.[17]

Putin will continue trying to impose a pro-Russian regime in Georgia, Moldova, and elsewhere. *Second*, as already noted, Biden made a surprise visit to Ukraine in February 2023. After his meeting with Zelensky, despite opinion polls showing that not only Republicans but American people in general want to stop providing huge sums and technology to Ukraine ad infinitum, Biden declared democracy must win "whatever it takes." *Third*, Xi Jinping declared that China may send arms to Russia. The American president reacted by pointing out that this is a *red line*. Subsequently a Chinese high placed official said that his country is against a nuclear war and wants negotiations.

In view of the above, we think that neither the revisionist Putin nor the crusader Biden have a solution to the present crisis. As to President Xi, he needs oil from Russia. Therefore, we think that the only peaceful solution is the one we have developed in Chapter 5.

Moving to the next crisis, after the visit of Nancy Pelosi (Speaker of the United States House of Representatives) to Taiwan in August 2022, China's reaction was immediate. There were Chinese military exercises around Taiwan and at the same time the Chinese government declared that any collaboration between China and the United States will stop.[18] That meant collaboration about how to deal with climate change, terrorism, and other global risks. For many observers, Pelosi's visit was dangerous. As is well known, China considers Taiwan as an integral part of its territory.

For some observers, President Xi intends to even use force, if the Ukrainian war continues. Meanwhile, the China-Russia relationship is getting stronger.

Concerning the Taiwan problem, many observers consider that it could lead to a global war. The problem is very complex. The great majority of Taiwanese people want de jure independence. As to the American position, it is characterized by "strategic ambiguity." In the sense that in case of a violent confrontation, the United States will provide arms and economic and technological assistance, but the US military will probably not be involved in military operations.

Enter the energy crises: Since 2020 the EU had devised an energy policy to adapt to the constraints of climate change. But starting in February 2022, the war in Ukraine provoked policy shifts. Briefly, the EU has set itself the goal to become carbon-neutral by 2050. It has also aimed to boost its own energy production, thus lessening dependency on non-EU energy producers. While the EU has not back-pedaled on the highly debatable nuclear energy production, on which some EU member states (e.g., France, Belgium) have long invested, it has tried to shift to renewable energies to make a transition from fossil fuels. Member states of the EU have committed themselves to reduce greenhouse gas emissions by 55 percent by 2030, compared to 1990 emission levels.[19]

There was an excess demand for natural gas in Europe in late 2021, as the Covid-19 pandemic subsided and European economies started recovering. The demand stimulated a rise in the price of natural gas, measured in euros per megawatt hour (MWh). The price rose sharply after Russia's invasion of Ukraine in February 2022, as the war provoked uncertainty about the adequacy of natural gas supply, while Russia also used energy supply as a political weapon against EU countries supporting Ukraine. Thus, the natural gas prices hit a record level of about €350/MWh in August 2022. An energy crisis was in sight, as the winter of 2022–3 approached.

Initially, in 2022 the EU member states adopted their own national policy responses to the crisis, practicing "energy nationalism." They competed for energy sources, while the EU initially failed to effect rules for security of energy supply and affordable energy prices. Eventually, in December 2022, an agreement was reached among EU member states on two fronts. First, a temporary emergency regulation was adopted to accelerate the production of renewables-based energy. Among other provisions, the regulation aimed at much faster than before permit procedures for solar equipment installations and renewable energy power plants. The agreement's implementation started in February 2023 and would last for 18 months.

Second, EU member states agreed to protect businesses and vulnerable households from the cost of exorbitant energy prices. They reached another temporary agreement, based on a "Market Correction Mechanism." The agreement entered into force in February 2023. The mechanism would be triggered off if the month-ahead Title Transfer Facility (TTF) price exceeded

€180/MWh for 3 working days and if the TTF price was €35 higher than a reference price for liquefied natural gas (LNG) on global markets for the same 3 working days.[20]

Energy prices started climbing down as the spring of 2023 approached (e.g., in late February 2023 the aforementioned TTF price was approximately €50/ MWh). In brief, the EU managed the energy crisis of the winter 2022–3, but it must prepare itself for the cold months of 2023–4 too. To that effect the EU has set the target that gas storage facilities should be 90 percent full by October 1, 2023. Meanwhile, Russia has signed many long-term contracts to provide gas to European countries and can weaponize gas flows anytime it chooses to do so. Finally, if EU wants to play the role of a megapower in the world economic and diplomatic order, it needs to continue a structural shift away from gas.

To close this chapter, in sum, it is concluded that the various crises had a serious impact on the EU. Concerning the economic crisis there was a set of positive policies like the creation of the European Financial Stability Facility and the support to member state bailouts. In this way the difference between more and less developed EU member states was narrowed, enhancing thus the EU's integration. As already mentioned, the pandemic crisis set off "vaccination nationalism," but later there were new EU interventionist policies that did not solve but alleviated the situation. As to the Ukrainian crisis, the EU suffered more from the conflict between Russia and NATO forces.[21] Because of this, there is more determination by EU member states to increase their military forces and at the same time to enhance their autonomy from the United States (e.g., President Macron emphasizes such autonomy). As to the energy crisis, here division prevailed over unity. Some EU member states (e.g., Germany) initially followed an "energy nationalism," but by late 2022 all member states converged on EU-wide measures.

Notes

1　For post-Fordism, see the edited volume by Amin (1994).
2　See Moschonas (2002).
3　See Duggan and Adams (2023).
4　See Colignon (2012).

5 According to David Beasley, executive director of the UN World Food Programme, 323 million people will be "marching toward starvation."

6 During the unification of Germany, the allies promised that there will be no extension of NATO to the East. This was ignored.

7 President Xi made no mention of Ukraine at all. He consciously withheld any public support for Putin's war.

8 India is buying grain from Russia. Biden's pressure to stop an India-Russia cooperation was not successful.

9 Sanctions entailed mainly freezing Russia's assets, banning the sale of high-tech components and excluding the country from the SWIFT, a global payment system. But they were not enough to completely undermine Russia's economy. This is obvious, if we take into account that Russia found ways to avoid sanctions (see *The Economist*, February 4, 2023).

10 EU leaders agreed to ban the majority of Russian oil imports. But Hungary, Slovakia, and the Czech Republic asked for an extension of the period during which they will continue to accept Russian exports.

11 President Biden decided to send advanced weapons to the Ukrainian fighters. On the other hand, however, he softened his previous critique against Putin. He moved from statements such as "we want to punish and weaken Russia" to "we do not want to prolong the war just in order to inflict pain on Russia." This "softening" changed later when a global confrontation occurred between the United States and China, which could provoke fears of a future nuclear war.

12 See Kissinger (2002) for this view on the Ukrainian crisis. Kissinger (2015) in his book *World Order*, among other interesting analyses, points out that there are two characteristics that lead to order in general: *common interests* and *common values*. In the case of global order, the two superpowers (the United States and China) have common interests. They both want to avoid a nuclear war and they are both in favor of legitimate economic competition leading to global growth. As far as values are concerned, given different cultures and historical developments, differences prevail. We think that Kissinger's position comes close to our idea of an institutionalized tripolar global governance of the United States, China, and the EU. These three actors represent the three capitalist subsystems of the globalized capitalist world. In view of the above, despite the differences in values, common interest prevails. The Chinese and the American presidents as well as EU's leaders realize that a cooperation between the three is the most important precondition for handling global risks like irreversible ecological destruction and a nuclear world war.

13 The argument is that the continuation of the war undermines green policies.

14 Another poll published in the *Wall Street Journal* found that whereas in March 2022 only 6 percent of Republicans said that the United States "was doing too

much" to support Ukraine, the percentage rose to 48 percent in November. But there are hawks both in Ukraine and in the United States believing that the only solution is the total defeat of Russia.

15 The Chinese president is also pressing for negotiations. He criticized Putin for his mistaken strategy, and he rejected a Russian-Chinese military cooperation. This changed later. China needs Russian petrol for its development.

16 In this list "denazification" is not mentioned, since in the 2019 parliamentary elections only 2 percent of votes went to far right groups.

17 When Russia was in desperate need of China, the latter refused Putin's proposal for a military cooperation between the two countries. Later, when China announced the possibility of sending arms to Putin, Russia stopped being a satellite and became China's partner. As we have already mentioned, later the situation changed again. By a second declaration, China, against the wishes of Russia, declared that she is against the use of nuclear weapons and for the start of negotiations.

18 However, later, China reopened her economic policy (see Chapter 3) and proposed cooperation on issues like climate change.

19 See European Commission-Energy (2022).

20 See details in Euronews (2022) and Euroactiv (2022).

21 The EU has suffered and continues to suffer more than the United States from the Ukrainian war. The United States is not only geographically distant from the war zone, but also relies on cheap energy sources, technological leadership, and a world reserve currency. In that sense Biden's protectionist policies may lead to a European deindustrialization. He offered important advantages to enterprises that will invest in the United States. Macron in his visit to the White House in December 2022 tried to persuade the American president to change his protectionist policies but he failed.

8

Social Democracy 2.0

In this chapter, we discuss European integration and the challenges that it has faced in the international scene since the economic crisis. We argue that the EU constitutes a social democratic subsystem of capitalism. Elevated to a meta-national level, social democracy can become partner of a new global arrangement to prevent and manage global risks in the twenty-first century.

The EU started with the creation of the European Coal and Steel Community established in 1951–with only six members (France, Italy, Luxemburg, the Netherlands, Belgium, and West Germany). It has now twenty-seven members while many more want to join, even though the EU Enlargement Process takes a long time to complete.[1]

The introduction of a common currency, the euro, in 1999 was a turning point. It enhanced the further strengthening of economic and political institutions. This process was accelerated by the UK's decision to opt out of the EU in 2016. Brexit strengthened European solidarity. This is evident, if one takes into account that Britain wanted a Europe-wide extended market. The UK did not care about further political integration. In the eyes of a considerable part of British political elites and the British electorate, taking orders from the so-called Brussels bureaucracy was a constant irritation.[2] In the eyes of some Europeans, with the benefit of hindsight, Charles De Gaulle was right in rejecting UK's request to join the EU.

Of course, at first the unification process was slow. During the 2008–9 economic crisis the central banks of EU member states managed to overcome the ensuing difficulties in a context where Germany imposed a strict financial regime. Economic austerity led to growing inequalities and the weakening of the welfare state. But following the pandemic crisis in 2020, the situation changed rapidly. The major breakthrough came with the Merkel-Macron agreement for the creation of the Recovery and Resilience Facility (RRF), a fund officially established in February 2021. This helped the EU less developed countries to cope with the difficulties of the Covid-19 pandemic. To a considerable extent, among other changes, it reduced the growing inequalities between the North and South of the EU. Inequalities during the pre-pandemic period occurred by mechanisms that were systematically transferring resources from the less to the more developed EU member states.

In 2020–2 the EU conservatives reacted negatively to the huge resources spent during the pandemic. Their argument was that this will create a huge public debt and will lead to inflation. However, for many observers the fear of high inflation was at that time unjustified. They argued that EU countries would soon reach precrisis levels of growth. Generally, we think that the shift from neoliberal to more interventionist forms of state regulation will continue. As during the social democracy's "golden years" (Chapter 6), meta-national social democracy will spread further political and social rights to the majority of European citizens. The present trend is definitely not to be reversed. We think that it will be difficult to return to a prepandemic "normality," taking into account any future repercussions of the ongoing Ukrainian war that since February 2022 has shaken the global social order.

In the sphere of rights, EU's Pillar of Social Rights has led to a relative reduction of poverty, unemployment, and the strengthening of collective agreements. Moreover, the Lisbon treaty (2009) gave legal effect to the Charter of Fundamental Rights. This basically consists of a catalog of rights against which the EU's legal acts can be judged. Here one should add the creation of the European Ombudsman (1992), an organization to which citizens may resort for the investigation of administrative malpractices, discrimination, and abuse of power. The EU has also legislation on sexual, racial, and workplace discrimination. In this context, it is not surprising that a UN report pointed out that EU countries, particularly Nordic ones, have achieved more equality, better public health, and high life expectancy. Because of the above, in 2012, the Nobel Prize was awarded to the EU, since it managed to transform most of Europe "from a continent of war to a continent of peace."

In the EU there has also been gradual cultural integration. Particularly among young Europeans, a common lifestyle has arisen. It has been propelled by the freedom of movement across the EU for young people holding the characteristic EU purple-colored passport and by the establishment of educational exchange programs, such as the popular among students "Erasmus" program.

There are other common grounds uniting Europeans at the practical and symbolic levels. At the practical level, EU citizens (all citizens of all EU member states) are entitled to hold and use the European Health Insurance Card, in order to benefit from emergency medical treatment and care when temporarily abroad. And they are also entitled to hold the same pink-colored driving license, valid and recognizable across the EU. At the symbolic level, the EU possesses a flag and a "national" anthem heard at major events broadcasted by the European Broadcasting Union (EBU), such as European-wide sports championships and song contests (the Eurovision).

Finally, in the sphere of civil society, the climate crisis and the pandemic have led to the development of self-help societies and NGOs demanding an acceleration of green policies and more help to those peripheralized by the pandemic. Moreover, a European social sphere has been created entailing grassroots organizations, cultural platforms, and civil society networks.

There were, of course, difficulties and drawbacks regarding EU integration. As already mentioned in Chapter 7, two countertrends have emerged: "vaccination nationalism" and "energy nationalism." Moreover, since the mid-2010s some of the North and Central European countries have reacted negatively to inflows of migrants. They refused to accept their share of migrants. Thus, the massive influx of migrants remained in the South. The European Trade Union Confederation (ETUC) has proposed an asylum system with equitable distribution of people seeking refuge among member states.[3] This was ignored.

Finally, apparently there is widespread corruption in the EU. In the winter of 2022–3 the Qatargate case, in which some members of the European Parliament were involved, was definitely a serious drawback. Europhobes started predicting the overall collapse of the European edifice. However, this is not the first crisis that the EU has faced. As in previous cases, this one will be tackled successfully. What is obviously needed is stricter regulations. A process that has already started. Many of the implicated politicians and their associates have been identified. They are already under criminal investigations.

Another difficult problem is the huge number of lobbyists who—with legal or illegal means—try to influence important EU officials and parliamentarians. The European Commission and the European Council must devise new mechanisms in order to tackle this problem. It will be difficult since lobbying is legal. But in the parliamentary context, unregulated and unmonitored lobbying tends to distort the decision-making process. It undermines democracy since powerful interests have much more influence than less powerful citizens or NGOs. More specifically, concerning EU lobbying regulation there is the *Transparency Register.* An available base referring to persons and organizations, which try to influence EU policies. Unfortunately, there is no obligation for lobbyists to register. Obviously not only should registration of all lobbyists become obligatory, but each lobbyist should give detailed information about their activities. There are no doubts that much stricter regulations about lobbying must be formulated soon.

Moving to the political party system, in 2021 the German federal elections led to the nomination of the social democrat Scholz as a chancellor and the formation of an alliance between the social democratic party (SPD), the Greens, and the Liberals. This had, of course, a considerable impact all over Europe. It led to the prevalence of social democracy in Nordic countries and to progressive developments in Portugal and Spain. All the above meant a considerable *social democratization of Europe.*[4] We see the spread of political, social, and cultural rights. Trade unions were somewhat strengthened, the minimum wage was raised in many countries, minorities were somewhat more protected, and the rights of people with different sexual orientations were reinforced.

Of course, there are also difficulties. France and Germany, the two major countries in the union, "have forgotten how to cooperate."[5] For instance, concerning the war in Ukraine, both want to support Zelensky, but in different ways. Moreover, while Macron wanted an EU joint borrowing of necessary funds to finance the cost of more expensive energy or for gas prices to be capped, Scholz followed initially an "energy nationalism" (see Chapter 7).

Finally, a compromise was reached. But basically, what Scholz wants is to go back to pre-Covid-19 EU budget rules.

Unfortunately, democratization has not prevented the further growth of authoritarian populism. This is not only happening in countries like Hungary and Poland. In 2022 in France the electoral influence of Marine Le Pen was high to the point of threatening Macron's reelection. Meanwhile, there was the formation of a tripartite far right populist government, under Georgia Meloni, in Italy. Populism is rising.

However, we think that there are four reasons that limit the power of rising populism in Europe. First, let us consider globalization. As is well known, globalization does not eliminate the nation-state, but it reduces its autonomy. It is not therefore surprising that populists are against globalization. They prefer deglobalization. As we have already mentioned (see Chapter 5), there are periods of deglobalization during crises (economic, pandemic, etc.) But overall, particularly if one focuses not only on the economic sphere, but also on the scientific, technological and cultural spheres, globalization does not stop. Given the growing interconnectivity of countries in global capitalism, knowledge, both theoretical and applied, spreads everywhere. The same is true in cultural terms. All over the globe and particularly in the megacities, consumerism, secularization, and individualistic models of life prevail.[6]

A second reason, which is undermining populist parties, consists of the huge funds that the EU transfers to its member states. The union has finally found ways not to tolerate governments that refuse to follow the rule of law and other liberal values.[7] For instance, in the case of Hungary, the European Commission refused to release a large part of the huge funds, which Hungary's populist government was expecting, because the Orban government policies were undermining the rule of law. Orban changed course and promised to shift his policies but did not keep his promise. So, the EU budget commissioner refused to give all the funds that Orban's government was expecting to receive. Moving to Italy, Prime Minister Meloni was obliged to tone down her neofascist discourse because of the risk of losing the "Next Generation EU" funds.

Third, EU's executive branch functions in an institutionalized anti-populist framework. Obviously, the European Commission's president, von der Leyen, and the rest of the top personnel of EU organs are not friends of populists like Meloni, Salvini, or Le Pen. At present populist parties do not want to have their countries exit the union. They prefer to remain in the EU and transform it from within, undermining EU's autonomy. But, as we have already mentioned, this is very difficult to do.

Finally, the fourth and most important reason for the incapacity of the rising populisms to undermine the EU is that, as we have already mentioned in Chapter 2, global capitalism is divided into three capitalist subsystems. The neoliberal is mainly represented by the United States, the authoritarian one is represented by China, and the social democratic one is represented by the EU. To a large extent the union is still social democratic, despite the fact that some of its member states are not. It combines a democratically elected parliament, a dynamic economy (at least before the Ukrainian crisis that led to high inflation in all member states), and a well-developed, state-led, welfare protection to citizens. It is for this reason that many countries want to join it. The EU does not have at present a strong European army but is an important player in the global arena.

Therefore, the union should not fear the rise of populism in various EU member states. This does not mean that further action is not needed. Anti-populist and antifascist mobilization by trade unions, NGOs, and other social movements are necessary;[8] as well as more alliances between left, social democratic, and liberal parties. What is also needed is more cooperation between France and Germany.

In the geopolitical sphere, in which the EU wants to play a role, the most striking development is that Western sanctions against Russia did not undermine seriously the Russian economy. Not only there was no collapse, but Russia's exports to India and China increased, to the extent that Russia has now a huge export surplus. How is this possible? We think that the West has not taken seriously into account China's present strength and the fact that the geopolitical balance of power between the West and the "rest" has changed in favor of the latter. Given the above tectonic change, games are played differently. What worked before does not necessarily work at present.

Within this new framework what are the EU relations with the United States and China? Concerning the former, Biden has managed to bring the EU closer to the transatlantic camp where American interests prevail. The EU members suffered more from the war in Ukraine than did distant America. Several EU member states were not able to cope quickly with the energy problem (see Chapter 7).

Moreover, Biden's advice to the union to adopt a more aggressive policy against China did not work. Fortunately, the EU as well as China did not want to disrupt their important economic relations.[9] And rightly so. As already mentioned, we think that a major obstacle to the achievement of cooperation between the two superpowers is the US ideological crusade against China.[10] A policy that started with Trump but, after some hesitation, was continued by Biden. The latter tried to stop the growth of China and the spread of its model in Africa and elsewhere by means of an ideological war. Biden focused on the total absence of human rights in China and the consequent suppression of obtrusive minorities by "reeducation" or more violent means. The oppression of the Chinese people by Xi's regime does exist and is very appalling. But Biden cannot change it. Given the strong roots of China's authoritarianism, possible changes can only come from within the regime. Any opposition from the outside simply reinforces it.

Of course, it is not only Biden who undermines a global cooperation. Putin's revisionist policy that aims at the revival of a new Soviet-like empire is the second major obstacle. In relation to this, the American president does not realize that his hostility against the Chinese giant increases the possibility of China supporting Putin's revisionism. President Xi, on the other hand, basically wants a stable global environment that would allow his country to pursue economic growth without using military means. He also wants to continue the China-EU relationship that has been favorable for both sides. And as we argued in Chapter 5, it could have made possible a tripolar global governance scheme or arrangement among the United States, China, and the EU. Given China's lack of political rights and US poor provision of social rights, the EU, as a force that has achieved the development of both political and social rights, could become a coordinator of a tripolar arrangement. To put it differently, an institutionalized arrangement among the United States, China, and EU players, which represent the three subsystems of present capitalism, is the only way to move from an overall catastrophe to global survival.

Kevin Rudd in an important article in *Foreign Affairs* argued that Biden, despite his ideological war against China (see Chapter 4), followed, in different contexts, a more cautious position vis-à-vis the Chinese president.[11] And the same is true about China's discourse. For instance, in November 2021 in a call between Xi and Biden, the latter stressed the need for common measures so that the lines of communication remain open. And the former considered this proposal a positive sign. Moreover, the American president in a speech at the

Asia Society in Washington in May 2022 said that competition between the two superpowers need not lead to conflict.

In other words, the two leaders use alternative discourses according to the audiences they address. It was not therefore surprising that certain analysts observed tentative progress in the relationship between the two superpowers. This is now far less possible because of the global confrontation (mentioned in Chapter 7), which is related to the Ukrainian crisis.

Commenting on the conditions before the global confrontation, Kevin Rudd proposed the concept of "managed strategic competition" to avoid catastrophic events that both superpowers want to avoid. More specifically he thinks that the United States and China must establish an understanding of each other's red lines, so that accidents are avoided. They must also focus less on military and more on economic and technological competition, as well as on issues of climate change and global financial stability.

All the above are difficult to achieve. But according to Rudd, in the context of "managed strategic competition," one should take into account that during the Cuban missile crisis in 1962 the United States and the Soviet Union agreed on a number of stabilizing arrangements that were related to the 1975 Helsinki accords that led to thirty years of strategic competition without a nuclear war.

We agree with the idea of a managed strategic competition. But our proposal for a China, US, and the EU tripolar governance is different. It goes beyond achieving the avoidance of a catastrophic miscalculation between the two superpowers. It stresses not only the avoidance of a nuclear confrontation, but also the capacity of the three global players to tackle effectively global risks, such as climate change for which, at present, no solution is in sight.

To sum up, the EU despite its cultural, political, and social diversities has achieved considerable integration via democratic means—an unprecedented phenomenon. Previous predictions about the EU's collapse have almost disappeared. At present the EU has become a major player in the global arena. This is not going to change in the years to come—at least not as long as capitalism survives (see Chapter 1).

The EU will not, of course, play a hegemonic role. It cannot and will not be able to set the basic rules of the future global social order. But we think that it can contribute to a US-China cooperation. In that sense the EU will influence future developments in a progressive manner. This will increase the possibilities of avoiding an ecological catastrophe, the continuation of a new cold war, and the possibility of a nuclear world war.

Of course, this does not mean that further transformation is not needed. The EU today is mainly (but not only) a huge market. It transcends national boundaries providing the free movement of goods, services, people, and capital. In that sense, given the purchasing power of almost half a billion European consumers, the union is a commercial giant. But in the political sphere it is still national governments that have the upper hand. Intergovernmentalism, rather than any type of federal model, prevails in EU's governance. In other terms, there is a marked imbalance between EU's integrated market and the relatively autonomous national governments of EU member states. This imbalance must be overcome by the gradual transfer of power to an EU post-national center leading thus to more integration. From the unification of the banking system till the idea of creating a federal Europe,[12] the union can become a superpower able to play the leading role in dealing with the climate crisis and with the present alarming confrontation between the United States and China.

Finally, moving to the geopolitical sphere, the union needs to attain more autonomy from both the United States and China. As Macron pointed out long ago, the EU needs "strategic sovereignty." At present the European Commission president von der Leyen follows faithfully Biden's policies. For instance, in April 2023, during the visit of herself and Macron to Beijing, the French president accepted several of the twelve points contained in China's proposal for ending the Ukrainian crisis. He also agreed with the Chinese president that the strict division between the two blocks and Biden's strategy of "decoupling" the two major economies lead to an impasse. It leads to lesser growth and the accentuation of the hostility between the two superpowers. Moreover, Biden's protectionist policies, as we have already mentioned, may lead to further deindustrialization of the union's economy. The EU should not become a satellite of the United States.

We close this chapter by discussing briefly the future of social democracy. Despite its present difficulties (growing inequalities, scandals, bureaucratization, populism, and other dysfunctions) *meta-national* social democracy will survive and develop further. For some analysts this is wishful thinking. Parties that call themselves social democratic or socialist may be declining in terms of their electoral influence in national elections. But if we take into account the *whole* of the EU, this is misleading.

In terms of (1) the union's institutional structure, (2) its relative help to less developed member states (e.g., by the creation of the RRF Fund), (3) the EU-wide gradual spread of civic, political, social, and cultural rights, (4) the growing capacity of EU organs to impose serious sanctions on member states which continue to resist the rule of law, there is a rebirth of social democracy at a post-national level, that is, the EU level. We think, thus, that the crisis of social democracy which started in the late 1970s can be overcome. Because of the EU and on the shoulders of the EU, social democracy today, which we call in this book "Social Democracy 2.0," can become a global power. In comparison with the two superpowers, the EU combines economic development with representative democracy and an extensive welfare state.

To that effect, it is time that France and Germany, the EU's most powerful member states, manage to cooperate. If nothing changes, the union may become a nonintegrated whole with several "failed regions." Germany is the strongest economic power in the EU. France, which has less economic but more political power, is the only EU member with nuclear weapons. There are other imbalances too that need to be redressed, not only at the EU, but at a global scale.

To conclude, in present-day capitalism there is an imbalance of power between those who mainly control the means of production, domination, and cultural influence and those who do not. Yet, capitalism, although not eternal, will be with us for a very long time still. If we take into account the above, social democracy, in Europe and elsewhere, is the only type of capitalism with a human face. Obviously, it will not shape the future, but it may attenuate the hostility between the two superpowers, a fundamental precondition for handling global risks.

Notes

1 See Hix (1999).

2 It was more than an irritation, if one takes into account that the British who, partly at least, won the Second World War had to take orders from the Germans who lost it.

3 For example, see the Statement of ETUC, published on December 8, 2021, "ETUC Statement on Belarus-EU border: Border guards, walls and razor

wire cannot be the response to a humanitarian emergency," https://www. etuc.org/en/document/etuc-statement-belarus-eu-border-border-gua rds-walls-and-razor-wire-cannot-be- response.

4 For the first time since 2001, five Nordic countries have social democratic governments. They try to reduce inequalities and to eliminate profit-oriented schools. But some of their politics are less social democratic. They tend to be against migrants and fail to reduce growing inequalities (see *The Economist*, January 22, 2022). Concerning democratization inside Germany, it entailed the establishment of minimum wages, more support of trade unions, and other quasi-Keynesian features. Such developments were due to Sakia Esken and Norbert Walter-Borjans, two left wing members who partly took the reins of the SPD party's organization.

5 See *The Economist*, October 29, 2022.

6 See Mouzelis (2021).

7 The European Court of Justice enhanced its ability to withhold funding to countries that ignore the rule of law. More specifically EU can impose sanctions when only a qualified majority of fifteen members agree.

8 An interesting move in that direction is the European Digital Public Sphere (EDPS). Its goals are to make knowledge generated by public funds to be digitally accessible to a broad public. For this to happen, there should be funding by members states in conjunction with new EU regulations.

9 To give an obvious example, the EU Commission hailed the EU-China *Comprehensive Agreement on Investment* (CAI). Owing to the tensions in Taiwan and the war in Ukraine, the EU decided to reassess the agreement. Given the above, Fu Cong (China's ambassador to the EU) has argued that European politicians should have the courage to ratify the CAI agreement. But ratification would mean that the EU would grossly diverge from the United States. We think that the Chinese ambassador is right. The EU should not follow what Biden demands. Following Macron's view, the union should have an autonomy from both the United States and China. The CAI agreement helps Europe and China. Europe should not become America's vassal. Particularly at a time when the American president follows a protectionist policy that encouraged European corporations to invest in the United States, leading to EU's deindustrialization.

10 Biden's ideological crusade failed. The EU in general and Germany in particular refused to follow the American advice. Many German corporations (particularly BMV, Mercedes, and Volkswagen) export 30–40 percent of their products to China. It is not therefore strange that the first European leader who visited China after the communist party's congress was Scholz.

11 See Rudd (2022).

12 See Tsoukalis (2022).

Part 4

The Future of Democracy

9

The Future of Democracy

After the Soviet Union's collapse, we observe a trend toward the demo-cratization of several countries. Fukuyama predicted that in the long term, democracy will lead to the "end of history."[1] Some years later, as the number of democratic regimes declined, Fukuyama realized that history's end is not coming or is never to come in the form he desired. By the beginning of the twenty-first century the rising number of new democracies came to a halt. There is evidence that since 2006 the number of political regimes in which government turnover occurs through democratic means has started declining.[2]

Given this, what are the causes of democracy's decline? According to Martin Wolf, the principal threat to Western democratic institutions comes not from China, but from our own societies.[3] In accordance with Wolf's position, many writers point at economic crises leading to stagnation, to growing inequalities related to the rise of populist parties, and to the working-class difficulties to adopt to new technologies, among other issues. But one can argue that inequalities, economic crises, and populist movements have also occurred in the past. But the type of decline that we see today in the democratic West did not occur.

Therefore, we think that putting the exclusive or main emphasis on the internal factors is not convincing. The weakening of Western democracies is more linked to the rise of China. To put it differently, without neglecting domestic factors that put democracy at risk in various countries, the decline was mainly due to *external pressures*,[4] particularly to the rapid globalization, as well as to China's entrance into the world markets. The combination of the abovementioned two developments led to China's extraordinary growth. As already mentioned (see Chapter 3), Chinese investments are spreading globally via the Silk Road, whereas its political model is expanding, particularly in poor countries that want to develop rapidly. In other words, overall globalization and the spread of China's political model has transformed radically the world. It has created a division between "the West and the rest." As a result, the democratic West is shrinking in comparison to the "rest." And this in a situation where in many poor countries people care less about democracy and more about getting out of poverty. (It is well known that absolute poverty has drastically declined in China.)[5]

Taking into account these developments, in explaining the democratic decline, there should be more emphasis on macro-historical developments, such as the rise of the Chinese giant that is not going to collapse or to become democratic, at least not in the short or medium run. This does not mean that China will unavoidably become the next hegemon. But its expansion cannot be stopped. The existing three capitalist subsystems will not converge since they need each other for their reproduction and further development (see Chapter 2). Nondemocratic political regimes may become more numerous in the decades to come. Any attempt by alliances based on American support to gradually democratize the world is going to fail.

Another development that preceded China's rise is the end of colonialism. This led to the relative independence of the colonized countries in Africa and Asia. The extraordinary power the colonizers had on the colonized declined. This also changed the geostrategic relation between the West and the rest of the world.

The way Big Tech private companies operate is also relevant when examining the future of democracy. There is no doubt that giant companies, such as Google, Amazon, Facebook, and Apple, rapidly pursue their own research in AI, robotics, digitalization, and other fields. By doing so, they have produced new knowledge and technologies. They have also enabled millions of users and customers to buy cheaper goods and services and also to communicate instantly with others living in any part of the globe.

On the other hand, Big Techs have also created very serious problems—political, economic, and social. To start with, their phenomenal profits enabled those who control them to acquire unprecedented political power. For instance, Mark Zuckerberg, Facebook's owner, is considered by many "the most powerful unelected individual in the USA." This may be an exaggeration, but it certainly shows how huge economic power can be easily transformed into political influence. Consider, for instance, the political influence that companies like Twitter (now renamed to "X") can exercise through shaping people's opinion all over the globe.[6] They can also collect data on individuals' ideas, preferences, and modes of life. This type of information, among other things, is sold to advertising firms. Therefore, it is not surprising that Big Techs can help powerful politicians to achieve goals such as winning elections or strengthening authoritarian regimes. In other words, there is a direct link between those who, to a great extent, control the means of communication and the decline of democratic institutions today.

Moving from the political to the economic sphere, Big Techs undermine competition.[7] They constitute, if not monopolies, surely oligopolies that compete but often cooperate with each other in quasi-secret ways. Needless to say, there have been attempts to combat monopolization. For instance, in the United States, via the already existing antitrust laws there were attempts to break up huge monopolies. The EU has also adopted legislation suitable to avert the creation of monopolies. But such attempts have not been successful. As for start-up companies, they are often incorporated into the Big Techs' domain. Another way to cope with the above problem is state regulation. But this method did not have much success—except in authoritarian regimes. For instance, in China, the government, when the Chinese Big Techs tried to go beyond the limiting framework imposed by the state, there was instant prohibition—since information in platforms criticizing governmental policies is forbidden.[8]

There is, of course, an argument developed by the Big Techs themselves about "auto-regulation." But this cannot happen, since there are obstacles to the organization of trade unions. For instance, Jeff Bezos, the Amazon's owner, undermines any attempts at resistance from below, that is, from among his employees. He has been accused of using illegal anti-union practices to undermine labor unions' power.[9] On the basis of the above, the Big Techs do provide useful services to common people. But at the same time, to a great extent, they also undermine democratic institutions all over the world.

To conclude this chapter, it is deduced that the decline of present democracies derives less from internal and more from external macro-historical developments, like the collapse of colonialism, rapid economic and technological globalization, and the rise of China. It is a global trend that will be difficult to reverse. But today the inadequate regulation of Big Techs can change for the better. Big Techs are formidable forces whose impact affects everyone. As we have already mentioned, these companies provide very useful services in terms of research, scientific breakthroughs, instant global communication, and cheap goods. But the currently available ways of regulating them are ineffective. They lead to massive tax evasion, global inequalities, and the concentration of economic, political and cultural power in the hands of the few. Among other ills, this state of affairs undermines democratic institutions.

Who can change the above dire situation? Surely neither the UN nor fragmented, local protests in distant corners of the world. It is only the three mega-actors, who mainly represent the three capitalist subsystems we examined in Chapter 2, the United States, China, and the EU, which can do so. If they cooperate in the construction of an institutionalized global governance (see Chapter 5), then they can create a framework that will oblige the Big Techs to curtail their damaging operations that affect democracy.

Notes

1 See Fukuyama (1992).
2 See Diamond (2015).
3 See Wolf (2022).
4 Internal causes are also relevant—but less so than macro-historical developments like the rise of China.
5 See The World Bank (2022).
6 Elon Mask, probably one of the richest men in the world, bought the Twitter (and renamed it to "X"). On this basis he has the power to manipulate financial markets. According to the *Economist* (April 23, 2022), the "Twitter saga in contemporary capitalism has gone rogue." Moreover, given that Musk believes in the "total freedom" of the media world, he can allow messages that can lead to racism, misogynism, and hatred. If one takes into account that millions of people are mainly or exclusively informed by giants like the Twitter, information instead of being a public good is regulated by private enterprises.
7 According to Cecilia Rikap (2023), huge American corporations like Microsoft constitute monopolies that transform national and transnational economies to the extent that they constitute a different type of capitalism.

8 For instance, the EU has created rules for regulating big-techs. But they are not effective (see *The Economist*, September 3, 2022). We think that only a global control by a tripolar governance (the United States, China, EU) can enforce such rules.

9 See Greenhouse (2023).

10

Conclusion

In Chapter 1 we have argued that particularly after the 2007–8 global crisis, several left-wing writers predicted the coming collapse of capitalism. They focused on *systemic contradictions rather than class struggles*. However, since its birth, capitalism has not succumbed to its internal contradictions. Any large-scale transformations of capitalism were owed to the way in which contradictions were related to collective actors. Given that today those who control the means of production, domination, and cultural influence are much stronger than the declining trade unions and other anti-capitalist forces, capitalism's collapse is not to happen. For instance, contradictions inherent to capitalism, such as the predicted capital's falling rate of profit, have not always taken place, nor could such contradictions, alone, spell the end of capitalism.

Our argument is that when one does not show in a theoretically congruent manner how contradictions are linked to collective actors, the former are transformed into anthropomorphic entities that, sooner rather than later, will allegedly lead to an overall capitalist breakdown. This is not convincing. Of course, capitalism is not eternal, but its disappearance is not around the corner.

In Chapter 2, we have argued that after the collapse of the Soviet Union, with very few exceptions, capitalism became global. It consists of three capitalist subsystems—the neoliberal represented mainly by the United States, the authoritarian capitalist subsystem whose main representative is China, and the European social democratic one. The latter denotes a balance between economic competitiveness, liberal democracy, and extensive welfare state.

The European capitalist subsystem is an emerging meta-national version of social democracy, as it is not confined within the boundaries of nation-states, but, in Europe at least, evolves at the level of the EU. And while the EU itself promotes the free-market model and capitalist investment, it does so in a manner that, from time to time and in certain policy sectors (e.g., environmental protection, business competition, gender equality in the workplace, personal data protection), seeks to curb the power of large businesses.

This sets contemporary European capitalism apart from the American and the Chinese one. None of the three capitalist subsystems is going to disappear. Of course, there might be at some point a new hegemon (according to many observers, China) setting the general framework for political and economic interaction among states and international organizations. But there will be no convergence. There will be neither Americanization nor sinicization of global capitalism. The three subsystems that have different logics and trajectories will persist, since they need each other for their reproduction and development.

In Chapter 3 we examined the rapid rise of China. In certain fields it is approaching the United States, whereas in others it is already ahead. China's economy is based on a combination of an authoritarian state focusing on rapid development and an economy where indigenous and foreign entrepreneurs have a relative autonomy. Provided they do not criticize the authoritarian character of the Chinese political regime, capitalist entrepreneurs turn a blind eye toward intraparty conflicts and accept various regulation measures. Despite the abovementioned difficulties, the huge Chinese market provides many opportunities and reasonable profits for entrepreneurs. Of course, there have been drawbacks and a slowing of the rate of growth, but on the whole, China continues its economic ascendance.

Politically in China there is a lot of repression. Trade unions have no autonomy, certain minorities are forcefully "reeducated," dissidents are brutally sanctioned, and the government fully controls almost everybody. On the other hand, despite huge income and asset inequalities in Chinese society, those at the base of the social pyramid have experienced some improvement whereas, at the same time, absolute poverty has been drastically reduced. As far as the middle class is concerned, there is a rapid growth but, unlike in other authoritarian regimes, there is no pressure "from below" for an opening of the political system.

Finally, ideologically there is a combination of Marxism and Confucianism—the latter stressing order, family, and the respect of ancestors as well as harmony in social relations. All these, plus an increasing nationalism on issues like the fate of Taiwan, legitimize the regime of the Chinese Communist Party (CCP) in the eyes of the Chinese people (internal legitimacy) and render it more stable than any other authoritarian government.

The spread of the Chinese model and its rapid expansion in Asia, Africa, and the Pacific region has brought a new divide between the "West and the rest," which once meant the contrast between the West and former European colonies. It now means the West versus China and its dependents, that is, countries tied to Chinese interests. We think that this tectonic change is irreversible.

In Chapter 4, we examined the US reaction to the rise of China. President Trump with his slogan "America first" followed a neoliberal policy at home and an aggressive foreign policy toward China. He also took distances from the EU. President Biden, on the other hand, has developed a progressive policy at home. His government not only has spent huge amounts of money on infrastructural investments but has supported poor families and the unemployed. There are also plans for the improvement of the American public educational and health systems.

In foreign affairs Biden started by stressing the need for legitimate competition rather than trade wars. However, soon Biden changed his policy and embarked on an ideological crusade against China's repressive features. He is also building alliances in order to stop the expansion of the Chinese model in other countries. This accentuates a growing hostility between the two superpowers and renders cooperation more difficult. For the moment, one observes a return to a new cold war as well as the simmering tensions between the United States and Russia. All these make it difficult to deal with global risks, such as climate change, pandemics, and nuclear threats.

In Chapter 5, we discuss the key issue of hegemony and global governance in the context of present-day globalization. Despite deglobalization tendencies during the two world wars and after, globalization has today reached its full extension. Big companies have penetrated all countries to the extent that their local brunches are to be found in most urban centers around the world. Moreover, via new information and communication technologies, people in different parts of the globe can have instant contact with relatives, friends, and colleagues.

The abovementioned developments raise the problem of global governance. Proposals for a global democratic governance for obvious reasons are utopian.

There are also predictions of a global authoritarian government by one of the two superpowers. This is also improbable. A third possibility, which we suggest in this book, is a three-side institutionalized co-governance among the United States, China, and the EU, each of which represents the three capitalist subsystems today.

Of course, this is a solution difficult to implement. But we think that there is no alternative, if we want to avoid nuclear wars, ecological destruction, and/ or catastrophic pandemics. Currently existing networks or bodies like the G7 and the G20 cannot provide global governance. It is only the United States and China that have enough economic, political, and geopolitical power to exercise global leadership, while the EU, the world's largest integrated market, could play the role of mediator, consensus-maker, and innovator.

In Chapter 6, our focus shifted from the global to the national level. During the early postwar period, social democratic governments, particularly in North-western Europe, developed policies that combined balanced economic growth, a developed welfare system, and democratic institutions. This led to the spread of civic, political, and social rights to the whole population. A situation that one can call "capitalism with a human face"—an unprecedented achievement. The system worked well till the opening of the world markets in the late 1970s. This changed the balance of power between labor and capital. From then on, entrepreneurs could transcend national boundaries whenever trade unions or governments tried to impose high taxes or other progressive policies. It is in this way that state autonomy was reduced. Social democratic parties, in order to survive, shifted to policies promoting almost unfettered economic competition and recalibrated the balance between capital and labor to the detriment of the latter. In other words, such parties had, to some extent, to adopt neoliberal policies.

Our story, as told in Chapter 7, attests to the demise of social democracy in the last quarter of the twentieth century. But one sees its resurgence in 2020–2, in the wake of the Covid-19 pandemic. After social democracy's crisis of the late 1970s, the next major one occurred in the 2007–8 period. Its negative effects spread all over the world. For some commentators, it resembled the stagflation of the 1970s.

However, there was a fundamental difference. In 2007–8 there was inflation, but not stagnation. The EU provided considerable financial support to EU member states. It bailed out countries undergoing severe economic crisis, particularly in the southern periphery of Europe, on the condition of implementing austerity policies. But as soon as the recovery was achieved, instead of continuing the fiscal stimulus, we saw a continuation to an austerity policy imposed by foreign creditors on the indebted countries in the early 2010s. That was a policy adopted and imposed by those who fear growing inflation.

On the other hand, during the Covid-19 pandemic in 2020–2, those who wanted a continuation of state interventionism for further growth (the European Council, the Biden administration in the United States) seem to have prevailed. As to the pandemic crisis, despite difficulties, the vaccination process progressed to the extent that in developed countries vaccines became available to all. However, in the poor countries, the opposite happened, widening the chasm between the capitalist center and the periphery.

Further on, as explained in Chapter 8, we witness a further transformation of social democracy. Social democracy will not signal the accentuation of the late twentieth century's neoliberal transformation, but rather its reversal. We call it "social democracy 2.0," in order to distinguish it from its twentieth-century variety. During the 1945–75 period, social democracy thrived within the boundaries of nation-states. It then shifted to neoliberalism. However, after the end of the Cold War the social democratic move to neoliberalism came to a halt. With the shift from the national to the meta-national level, the EU succeeded in overcoming its stagnation crisis, continuing thus the achievements of social democracy's golden period. Particularly after the Brexit, there was more EU integration as well as the further strengthening of civil, political, and social rights via the creation of new institutions and processes (e.g., the Recovery and Resilience Facility in 2020).

Needless to say, the transition from social democracy 1.0 to social democracy 2.0 was accompanied by further problems, such as the accentuation of populism and the refusal of Hungary and Poland to accept the rule of law and the EU basic values and rules. There are attempts by the EU to impose sanctions on these two EU member states. Until the government change of 2023 in Poland, the Polish government threatened a Polexit, but the majority of Poles wanted to stay in the union. As with previous crises of the EU, we think that the present difficulties will be overcome.

The social democratic EU may perhaps become the third global actor after China and the United States, if it measures up to the challenges of democracy that we surveyed in Chapter 9. In the last quarter of the twentieth century and certainly after the collapse of the Soviet Union, the number of democracies increased. Fukuyama predicted "the end of history." Among other things, he meant that liberal democracy would spread widely. This did not happen, rather the opposite. For some observers, democracy's decline is due to internal reasons—to the rise of populism, the depoliticization of citizens, the distance that social elites have taken from the social conditions and lifestyle of the middle and lower strata, the sense of unaccountability of political elites, and the weakening of democratic values and institutions.

This approach is useful only to a limited extent. It focuses on domestic developments in Western democracies. It underestimates the crucial importance of external developments, mainly, the end of colonialism, rapid economic and technological globalization, and later the rise of China and the spread of its model in the non-Western world. From this point of view, Fukuyama's prediction, as he himself admitted later, was wrong. Western democracies will survive, but authoritarian regimes may become more numerous.

The book's overall argument is based on the idea that today one cannot understand the European social democratic trajectory without paying serious attention to the overall development of capitalism, its chances of survival, its differentiation into three interrelated capitalist subsystems, and the overall character of present globalization. Therefore, when one examines political and social developments within the EU, problems of hegemony and global governance become crucial. In other words, the European road is to a great extent shaped by the rise of China, the confrontation with the United States, and the chances of dealing effectively with global risks. These are risks in a context where all countries are so closely interrelated that pandemics, ecological destruction, a third world war, and other calamities cannot only affect certain groups or countries. They will affect all countries and certainly the three largest players—the United States, China, and the EU. The risks are high for them too. They cannot manage them on their own. They thus have an incentive to seek cooperation with one another.

In that sense, we all share the same goal and the same destiny. We are obliged to be involved in an attempt to achieve survival. To put it differently, we find ourselves in a context where there can be no winners and losers. The game is for all either a "win-win" or a "lose-lose" one.

Marx argued that in the case of religion we created forces that led to alienation, that is, forces that turned against the common people. Today we have a different kind of alienation, a geopolitical one that may lead to destruction. People may be alienated, that is, indifferent to and clueless about global risks, while simultaneously the three global protagonists, the United States, China, and the EU, may be too preoccupied with their own economic and diplomatic three-way competition. As a result, they may not notice, let alone manage, the risks affecting all of them.

Therefore, the key question is how to avoid a total annihilation. We have argued that a fundamental precondition for avoiding the worst scenario of global risks is the creation of an institutionalized, hegemonic tripolar governance by the major representatives of the three capitalist subsystems: the United States, China, and the EU. These are the only forces that can create a framework within which, via incentives and penalties, all countries, organizations, and networks would contribute to the salvation of the planet.

Of course, some believe that there is another way to tackle global risks. According to them, global survival can only be achieved by an anti-capitalist revolution. But as we have argued in Chapter 1, although capitalism is not eternal, it will not collapse soon. Still others argue that in the context of the Covid-19 crisis they were not all losers; some few were clearly winners—for instance, pharmaceutical companies that, by refusing to waive their property rights, earned billions. This is true. But to repeat, further ecological destruction or a nuclear war will not allow for losers and winners; it will only produce losers.

Another argument against the idea of tripolar governance is that the "three hegemons" will focus more on their own common interests and less on the interests of all. However, if the hegemonic global governance scheme or tripolar arrangement follows such an authoritarian policy, it will have to face the opposition of other powerful states like India and Japan. This would lead to an impasse. To an impossibility to tackle global risks.

As long as capitalism does not collapse, the EU-like social democracy is the only capitalism with a human face. This social democracy cannot transform the world. But it can help the two superpowers (China and the United States) to move from the present growing confrontation to cooperation. Cooperation being the only way to cope effectively with global risks. Therefore, fighting for social democracy gives *meaning* to those who hope for a safer and better social world.

References

Albrow, M. (1990). *Max Weber's Construction of Social Theory*. London: Macmillan.

Alison, G. (2017). *Destined for War: Can America and China Escape Thucydides' Trap?* Boston: Houghton Mifflin Harcourt.

Amin, A. (1994). *Post-Fordism: A Reader*. Oxford: Blackwell.

Badiou, A. (2008). "The Communist Hypothesis." *New Left Review*, 49, 29–42.

Badiou, A. (2009). *Theory of the Subject*. London: Bloomsbury..

Badiou, A. (2010). *The Communist Hypothesis*. New York: Verso.

Badiou, A., and M. Gauchet (2016). *What Is to Be Done?: A Dialogue on Communism, Capitalism, and the Future of Democracy*. Maiden, MA: Polity.

Bailey, D. (2009). *The Political Economy of European Social Democracy*. New York: Routledge.

Barnett, J., J. Pevehouse, and C. Raustiala, eds. (2022). *Global Governance in a World of Change*. Cambridge: Cambridge University Press.

Bledsoe, E. (2023). "How Many US Military Bases Are There in the World?." *TheSoldiersProject*, September 1, https://www.thesoldiersproject.org/how-many-us-military-bases-are-there-in-the-world/, accessed on January 8, 2024.

Castells, M. (2010). *The Rise of the Network Society*, vol. 1, 2nd edition. Chichester: J. Wiley and Sons.

Clifford, P. G. (2021). *The China Paradox: At the Front Line of Economic Transformation*, 2nd edition. Boston: De Gruyter.

Cohen, R. (2023). "From Red Carpet to Doghouse: Macron Returns from China to Allied Dismay." *The New York Times*, April 11.

Colignon, S. (2012). "Europe's Debt Crisis, Coordination Failure, and International Effects." ADBI Working Paper no. 370, July, https://www.adb.org/sites/default/files/publication/156225/adbi-wp370.pdf, accessed on January 8, 2024.

Colomer, J. M. (2014). *How Global Institutions Rule the World*. New York: Palgrave Macmillan Press.

Colomer, J. M., and A. L. Beale (2020). *Democracy and Globalization: Anger, Fear and Hope*. London: Routledge.

Diamond, L. (2015). "Facing Up the Democratic Recession." *Journal of Democracy*, 26(1), 141–56.

Dikötter, F. (2022). *China after Mao: The Rise of a Superpower*. London: Bloomsbury.

Doerr, J. (2018). *How Google, Bono, and the Gates Foundation Rock the World with OKRs*. New York: Penguin.

Duggan, W., and M. Adams (2023). "A Short History of the Great Recession." *Forbes Advisor*, June 21, https://www.forbes.com/advisor/investing/great-recession/, accessed on January 8, 2024.

Esping-Andersen, G. (1990). *Three Worlds of Welfare Capitalism*. Princeton: Princeton University Press.

Euroactiv (2022). "EU Chief Lays out Five Measures to Tackle Energy Crisis." September 7, https://www.euroactiv.com/section/energy/news/eu-chef-lays-out-five-measures-to-tackle-energy-crisis/, accessed on January 8, 2024.

Euronews (2022). "Energy Crisis: Ursula von der Leyen Unveils Five Proposals to Curb Soaring Prices." September 8, https://www.euronews.com/my-eur ope/2022/09/07/europes-energy-crisis-ursula-von-der-leyen-unveils-five-propos als-to-curb-soaring-prices, accessed on January 8, 2024.

European Commission-Energy (2022). "What the European Commission Is Doing." https://ec.europa.eu/info/topics/energy, accessed on January 8, 2024.

Frieden, J., and R. Rogowski (2014). *The Spread of Capitalism: From 1848 to the Present*. Cambridge: Cambridge University Press.

Friedman, M. (1962). *Capitalism and Freedom*. Chicago: University of Chicago Press.

Fukuyama, F. (1992. *The End of History and the Last Man*. New York: Penguin.

Garton, Ash T. (1999). *We the People. The Revolution of '89 Witnessed in Warsaw, Budapest, Berlin and Prague*. London: Penguin.

Gillingham J. R. (2016). *The EU: An Obituary*. London: Verso.

Gindin, S., and L. Panitch (2012). *The Making of Global Capitalism: The Political Economy of American Empire*. New York: Verso.

Goldberg, P., and T. Reed (2023). "Is the World Economy Deglobalizing? And If So, Why? And What Is Next?." Brooking Papers on Economic Activity, March. https://www.nber.org/papers/w31115, accessed on January 8, 2024.

Greenhouse, S. (2023). "'Old-School Union Busting': How US Corporations Are Quashing the New Wave of Organizing." *The Guardian*, February 26.

Hall, P. A., and D. Soskice (2001). *Varieties of Capitalism: The Institutional Foundations of Comparative Advantage*. Oxford: Oxford University Press.

Hardt, M., and A. Negri (2000). *Empire*. Cambridge, MA: Harvard University Press.

Hardt, M., and A. Negri (2004). *Multitude: War and Democracy in the Age of Empire*. New York: Penguin.

Hasenclever, A., P. Mayer, and V. Rittberger (1997). *Theories of International Regimes*. Cambridge: Cambridge University Press.

Harvey, D. (2010). *The Enigma of Capital: And the Crises of Capitalism*. New York: Oxford University Press.

Held, D. (1995). *Democracy and Global Order: From the Modern State to Cosmopolitan Governance*. Cambridge: Polity.

Held, D. (2017). "Elements of a Theory of Global Governance." *Glocalism*, 2(1), 1–14.

Hix, S. (1999). *The Political System of the European Union*. London: Palgrave.

Hung, H. F. (2009). *China and the Transformation of Global Capitalism*. Baltimore: Johns Hopkins University Press.

Irwin, N. (2020). "The Pandemic Is Showing Us How Capitalism Is Amazing, and Inadequate." *The New York Times*, November 14, https://www.nytimes.com/2020/11/14/upshot/coronavirus-capitalism-vaccine.html, accessed on January 8, 2024.

Jackson, T. (2021). *Post-Growth: Life after Capitalism*. Cambridge: Polity Press.

Jain-Chandra, S., N. Khor, R. Mano, J. Schauer, Ph. Wingender, and J. Zhuang (2018). "Inequality in China." IMF Working Paper WP/18/127. Washington, DC: IMF.

Johnson, Ch. (2004). *Sorrows of Empire: Militarism. Secrecy and the End of the Republic*. New York: H. Holt and Co.

Johnson, Ch. (2007). *Nemesis: The Last Days of the American Republic*. New York: Metropolitan Books.

Kirshner, J. (2012). "The Tragedy of Offensive Realism: Classical Realism and the Rice of China." *European Journal of International Relations*.

Kissinger, H. (2015). *World Order*. London: Penguin.

Kissinger, H. (2022). "How to Avoid Another World War." *The Spectator*, December 17, 2022, https://www.spectator.co.uk/article/the-push-for-peace/, accessed on January 8, 2024.

Korpi, W. (1983). *The Democratic Class Struggle*. London: Routledge and Kegan Paul.

Krastev, I. (2020). *After Europe*. Philadelphia: University of Pennsylvania Press.

Krippner, G. R. (2005). "The Financialization of American Economy." *Socio-Economic Review*, 3(2), 173–208.

Kucik, J. (2021). "How Trump Fueled Economic Inequality in America." *The Hill*, January 21, 2021, https://thehill.com/opinion/finance/535239-how-trump- fueled-economic-inequality-in-america/, accessed on January 8, 2024.

Laclau, E. (2005). *On Populist Reason*. London: Verso.

Lemert, C., A. Elliott, D. Chaffee, and E. Hsu, eds. (2010). *Globalization: A Reader*. London: Routledge.

Lockwood, D. (1964). "Social Integration and System Integration." In: *Explorations in Social Change*, G. K. Zollschan and W. Hirsch (eds.). London: Routledge, pp. 370–83.

Mann, M. (1986). *The Sources of Social Power, Vol. 1.* Cambridge: Cambridge University Press.

Mann, M. (1993). *The Sources of Social Power, Vol. II: The Rise of Classes and Nation-States, 1760–1914.* Cambridge: Cambridge University Press.

Marshall, T. H. (1964). *Class, Citizenship and Social Development.* New York: Doubleday.

Mathews, J. T. (2017). "Can China Replace the West?." *The New York Review of Books*, May 11, https://www.nybooks.com/articles/2017/05/11/easternization-can-china-replace-the-west/, accessed on January 8, 2024.

Mazzucato, M. (2013). *The Entrepreneurial State: Debunking Public vs. Private Sector Myths.* London: Anthem Press.

Milanovic, B. (2016). *Global Inequality: A New Approach to the Age of Globalization.* Cambridge, MA: Belknap Press.

Mitter, R. (2016). *Modern China: A Very Short Introduction.* Oxford: Oxford University Press.

Moschonas, G. (2002). *In the Name of Social Democracy. The Great Transformation, 1945 to the Present.* London: Verso.

Mould, O. (2018). *Against Creativity.* London: Verso.

Mouzelis, N. P. (1986). *Politics in the Semi-Periphery: Early Industrialization and Late Parliamentarism in Latin America and the Balkans.* London: Macmillan.

Mouzelis, N. (1997). "Social and System Integration: Lockwood, Habermas, Giddens." *Sociology*, 31(1): 111–19.

Mouzelis, N. P. (2021). *Religious and Ethical Perspectives.* Champaign, IL: Common Ground Research Networks.

Nye, J. (2005). *Soft Power: The Means to Success in World Politics.* New York: Public Affairs Books.

Nye, J. (2015). *Is the American Century Over?* Cambridge: Polity.

Parsons, T. (1951). *The Social System.* New York: The Free Press.

Pearson, M., M. Rithmire, and K. S. Tsai (2021). "Party-State Capitalism." *Current History*, September, 120(827), 207–13.

Pew Research Center (2021). "How America Changed during Donald Trump's Presidency." January 21, 2021, https://www.pewresearch.org/2021/01/29/how-america-changed-during-donald-trumps-presidency/.

Piketty, T. (2014). *Capital in the Twenty First Century.* Cambridge, MA: Harvard University Press.

Piketty, T. (2022). "It Is Impossible to Seriously Fight Climate Change without a Profound Redistribution of Wealth." *Le Monde*, November 5, https://www.lemo nde.fr/en/opinion/article/2022/11/05/thomas-piketty-it-is-impossible-to-seriou sly-fight-climate-change-without-a-profound-redistribution-of-wealth_6003038_ 23.html, accessed on January 8, 2024.

Pirie, I. (2008). *The Korean Developmental State: From Dirigisme to Neo-liberalism*. London: Routledge.

Przeworski, A. (1985). *Capitalism and Social Democracy*. Cambridge: Cambridge University Press.

Rikap, C. (2023). "Capitalism as Usual?." *New Left Review*, 139, January/February, https://newleftreview.org/issues/ii139/articles/capitalism-as-usual, accessed on January 8, 2024.

Rodrik, D., and S. Walt (2021), "How to Construct a New Global Order." Harvard University, Kennedy School, https://drodrik.scholar.harvard.edu/files/dani-rodrik/ files/new_global_order.pdf.

Romers, P. M. (1990). "Endogenous Technological Change." *Journal of Political Economy*, 98(5): 70–102.

Romers, P. M. (1994). "The Origins of Endogenous Growth." *Journal of Economic Perspectives*, 8(1): 3–22.

Rudd, K. (2022). "The World According to Xi Jinping: What China's Ideologue in Chief Really Believes." *Foreign Affairs*, November–December, https://www.for eignaffairs.com/china/world-according-xi-jinping-china-ideologue-kevin-rudd, accessed on January 8, 2024.

Rueda, D. (2007). *Social Democracy Inside Out: Partisanship and Labor Market Policy in Advanced Industrialized Democracies*. Oxford: Oxford University Press.

Sassoon, D. (1996), *One Hundred Years of Socialism: The West European Left in the Twentieth Century*. London, Fontana Press.

Schmitter, Ph. C. (1974). "Still the Century of Corporatism?." *The Review of Politics*, 36(1), 85–131.

Streeck, W. (2014). How Will Capitalism End?." *New Left Review*, 87, 35–64.

Streeck, W. (2016). *How Will Capitalism End? Essays on a Failing System*. London: Verso.

Streeck, W. (2017). "The Return of the Repressed." *New Left Review*, 104, 5–18.

Tao, A. (2022). "Olaf Scholz's China Gamble." *The Diplomat*, December 21, https:// thediplomat.com/2022/12/olaf-scholzs-china-gamble/, accessed on January 8, 2024.

Therborn, G. (2021). "Inequalities and World–Political Landscapes." *New Left Review*, May/June, https://newleftreview.org/issues/ii129/articles/goran-therborn-inequality-and-world-political-landscapes, accessed on January 8, 2024.

Trimberger, K. E. (1978). *Revolution from Above: Military Bureaucrats and Development in Japan, Turkey, Egypt, and Peru.* New Brunswick, NJ: Transaction Books.

Tsoukalis, L. (2022). *Europe's Coming of Age.* New York: J. Wiley.

Unger, R. M. (2022). *Governing the World without World Government.* London: Verso.

Vartan, S. (2022). "Carbon Emissions by Country: Top 15." *Treehugger*, August 2, data form 2019 based on OurWorldinData.org, https://www.treehugger.com/greenhouse-gas-emissions-by-country-5120253, accessed on January 8, 2024.

Vesoulis, A. (2020). "12 Ways the Trump Administration Has Deepened Inequality." *Time Magazine*, June 25, https://time.com/5859209/donald-trump-administration-inequality/, accessed on January 8, 2024.

Wallerstein, I. (1974). *The Modern World System, Vol. I: Capitalist Agriculture and the Origins of the European World-Economy in the Sixteenth Century.* New York: Academic Press.

Wallerstein, I. (2013). "Structural Crisis, or Why Capitalists May No Longer Find Capitalism Rewarding." In: *Does Capitalism Have a Future?*, I. Wallerstein, R. Collins, M. Mann, G. Derluguian, and C. Calhoun (eds.), 18–57. Oxford: Oxford University Press.

Williamson, O. E. (1983). *Markets and Hierarchies: A Study in the Economics of Internal Organization.* New York: Free Press.

Wolff, M. (2022). *The Crisis of Democratic Capitalism.* London: Penguin.

World Bank (2022). "Four Decades of Poverty Reduction in China: Drivers, Insights for the World and the Way Ahead." Washington, DC: The World Bank, https://openknowledge.worldbank.org/server/api/core/bitstreams/e9a5bc3c-718d-57d8-9558-ce325407f737/content, accessed on January 8, 2024.

Xai, C. (2022), "The Weakness of Xi Jinping: How Hubris and Paranoia Threaten China's Future." *Foreign Affairs*, September/October, https://www.foreignaffairs.com/china/xi-jinping-china-weakness-hubris-paranoia-threaten-future, accessed on January 8, 2024.

Name Index

Africa 22, 24, 33, 67, 81, 90, 97
Amazon 7, 13, 90–1
Asia 23–4, 27, 33–4, 37, 82, 90, 97

Badiou, A. 8
Biden, J. 12–13, 16, 21, 24, 32–7, 43, 46,
    48–9, 65–70, 80–1, 83, 97, 99
Bourdieu, P. 16
Brexit 75, 99

China 1–2, 6, 9, 11–16, 19, 21–6, 31–7,
    41–3, 45–9, 51, 62, 65–70, 80–3, 89–92,
    95–8, 100–2
Chinese Communist Party (CCP) 23–5,
    96
Confucianism 9, 12, 96
COP 26 1, 45
COP 27 1, 45

Draghi, M. 14

Euro 14, 64, 71, 75
European Central Bank (ECB) 14,
    64
European Union (EU) 1–2, 7, 11, 13–14,
    16, 26, 31–7, 41, 43–6, 49, 51, 64–7,
    71–2, 75–84, 91–2, 95, 97–101
Eurozone 13, 64, 66

G7 1, 15, 47, 49, 65, 67, 98
G20 1, 15, 49, 98
Germany 16, 22, 35–6, 46, 65, 68, 72, 75,
    78, 80, 84
Google 7, 90

Hardt, M. 8
Harvey, D. 8
Hungary 78–9, 99

Keynesian, policies 13, 63

Latin America 11
Le Pen, M. 14

Macron, E. 14, 16, 32, 36, 66, 72, 75,
    78–9, 83
Marx, K. 5–6, 12, 25, 57, 96, 101
Marxism 12, 25, 96
Merkel, A. 14, 16, 35, 65, 75

NATO, 26, 31–2, 60–6, 68–9, 72
Negri, A. 8

Pacific (the) 32–3, 36–7, 69, 97
Poland 79, 99
Polanyi, K. 5
Putin, V. 16, 26–7, 36, 48–9, 66–70, 81

Resilience and Recovery Fund (RRF) 14,
    76, 84, 99
Russia 22, 26, 32, 36, 44, 48–9, 57, 65–72,
    80, 97

Salvini, M. 14, 79
Silk Road 9, 22, 37, 89
Sombart, W. 5
South Korea 11
Soviet model/regime 7–8, 11, 21, 25,
    66, 68, 81
Soviet Union 5, 25, 44, 46, 66, 68, 82, 89,
    95, 100
Streeck, W. 5–6, 8

Taiwan 24, 46, 63, 70, 96
Trump, D. 12–13, 16, 31–7, 43, 81, 97

Ukraine 16, 26, 66–8, 71, 78, 80
United Nations (UN) 1
United States of America (USA) 1, 11–16,
    21, 23–4, 26, 31–3, 36–7, 41–3, 45–9, 51,
    61–2, 66–70, 72, 80–3, 91–2, 95–102

Wallerstein, I. 7–8, 15, 44
West (the) 15, 26, 33–7, 41–2, 46, 65, 67–8,
     80, 89–90, 100

World Health Organization (WHO) 15

Xi, J. 24–7, 34, 37–8, 46, 49, 66, 70, 81

Subject Index

actor, -s 5–6, 8, 15, 41, 53, 45, 47–8, 50–1, 59, 92, 95, 100
agency 6, 59
army 9, 12, 14, 23, 27, 80
austerity 58, 64, 75, 99
autonomy 5–6, 21, 24–5, 32, 34–6, 69, 75, 79, 83, 96, 98
    strategic 14, 21, 66

capital 5–7, 13, 41, 44, 58, 60, 83, 98
    cultural 16
    financial 41
class struggle 6, 95
climate change 1–2, 32, 45–8, 70–1, 82, 97
communism 8
crisis, -es 2, 13–15, 22, 25, 63–6, 68, 70–2, 77, 84, 95, 98–9, 101
    climate 17, 77, 83
    economic 5, 58, 64, 72, 75–6, 99
    Ukrainian 23, 27, 36, 44, 66, 70, 72, 77, 82
culture 12, 22, 25, 38, 47

decarbonization 16, 45
democracy 2, 13, 46, 48, 50, 67–8, 70, 78, 84, 89–92, 95, 100
democratization 14, 16, 46, 48, 67, 78, 89
development 5–9, 11, 21, 21–2, 25–6, 32, 34–5, 37, 42–3, 48, 58–61, 66, 69, 77–8, 81–4, 89–91, 96–7, 100

election, -s 12, 78–9, 84, 91
elite, -s 9, 22, 38, 61, 75, 100
environment 23, 86, 91

gender 59, 96
globalization 2, 7–8, 13, 16, 33–4, 37, 41–9, 63, 66, 79, 89–91, 97, 100
growth 2, 5, 9, 11–14, 21–6, 31, 33–4, 37–8, 43, 47–9, 65–6, 76, 78, 81, 83, 89, 96, 98–9

hegemon, -y 2, 16, 21–3, 26, 31–4, 41–3, 46–8, 82, 90, 96–7, 100–1

inequality, -ies 6, 8–9, 11–12, 22, 26, 31, 35, 45, 58–9, 64, 75–6, 83, 89, 92, 96
integration
    European 13–14, 41, 64, 72, 74, 76–7, 82–3, 99
    social 59–60
    system 59, 61

labor 5–8, 13, 5, 60, 91, 98
legitimacy 12, 23, 24, 97
liberalism 42

market, -s 5–8, 11–14, 26, 49–50, 58, 60, 63, 71–2, 75, 83, 89, 95–6, 98
middle class, -es 9, 11, 23, 38, 58, 96, 100
minorities, ethnic 9, 12, 23, 31, 34, 38, 78, 81, 96
mode of production 6–7, 45
movements, social 5, 7–8, 23, 34, 41, 45, 80, 89

nation-state 1, 5, 8, 13, 41, 79, 91, 99
nationalism 9, 37, 64, 71–2, 77–8, 96
neoliberalism 99
non-governmental organizations (NGOs) 8, 77–80

pandemic, s 1–2, 7, 14–15, 34, 44, 47, 63–6, 71–2, 75–9, 97–100
patriotism 12, 24
periphery 7, 15, 27, 33, 44, 47, 51, 58, 77, 99
political party, -ies 11–12, 14, 23–5, 27, 57, 78, 96
populism 8, 79–80, 93, 99–100
poverty 24, 65, 101, 96–7, 99

rights 58, 60–1, 76, 78
    civil 60, 84, 98–9

cultural 78, 84
economic 98
gender 38
human 24, 38, 61, 81
political 59–61, 76, 78, 81, 84, 98–9
property 24, 65, 101
social 13, 46, 57–9, 76, 78, 81, 84, 98–9

sinicization 15, 34, 96
stagflation 6, 13, 63, 98
state 6–9, 13–15, 21–2, 24–5, 31–2, 38, 42,
     44, 46–7, 49, 57–8, 64, 67, 75, 76, 80,
     84, 91–2, 95–6, 98–9, 101
structure 1, 7, 9, 25, 47, 84
superpower, -s 9, 16, 21, 27, 33–7, 42–7, 62,
     69, 81–4, 97–8, 102
sub-system, -s, 2, 11–16, 34, 43, 45, 60–3,
     75, 80–1, 95–6, 90, 92, 95–6, 98, 100–1
system 5–9, 11–13, 21, 25–7, 33–4, 37,
     41–5, 47, 58–9, 61, 63, 77–8, 83, 96–8

tax, -es 12–13, 31, 92, 98

trade unions 5–9, 12, 34–5, 58, 60, 77–80,
     91, 95–6, 98

vaccination, -s 15, 64–5, 72, 77, 79
vaccines 15, 64–5, 99

War 33–8, 43–4, 49, 68–70, 76, 81, 97
     Cold 16, 36, 68, 83, 97, 99
     Nuclear 1–2, 15, 36, 44–50, 66–71, 82–4,
          97–8, 101
     Second World 32–3, 42, 44, 50, 57, 68
     Third World 16, 34, 48, 50, 67–8, 100
     Ukrainian 26, 46, 67–71, 76, 78, 80
wealth 6, 12, 23, 25, 45
weapon, -s 16, 36–7, 48, 66–9, 71, 84
welfare state 12–13, 38, 57–60, 64, 75, 80,
     84, 95, 98
world 1, 5, 7, 9, 11, 13, 15, 21–2, 23–6,
     31–7, 41–51, 58, 62–5, 67, 72, 89–91,
     97–8, 100, 102
     developed 15, 23
     developing 7, 23

www.ingramcontent.com/pod-product-compliance
Lightning Source LLC
Chambersburg PA
CBHW062042270326
41929CB00014B/2512